The Fiduciary Guide©

Chapters

1) What is a Fiduciary?

2) Power of Attorney

3) Trusts and Trustees

4) Conservator

5) Personal Representative/Executor

6) Guardian

7) Healthcare Representative

8) Advanced Directives

9) Case Management by a Fiduciary

10) Ethics of a professional fiduciary

Glossary

Bibliography

Introduction

There is a new industry that is rapidly evolving. It is the industry of a professional fiduciary. A fiduciary is someone placed into a position of trust – to manage either the finances of someone else, or to actually manage the 'someone else.' Chapter one will explain more about fiduciary roles and definitions, and this book will cover a multitude of examples and cases to give the new or experienced fiduciary a solid understanding of what is expected of them.

In 1978, I started my professional career in credit unions, starting as a loan file clerk for a very large credit union in Sacramento, California. Over the next 23 years, I advanced through the ranks to eventually become a Chief Financial Officer for a large credit union in Eugene, Oregon. I was at the peak of my career, positioned to be the Chief Executive Officer and President of either that credit union of which I was employed, or another at my choosing.

Then, it happened.

My wife, Rikki, started a small company in 1999 called Cornerstone Services, Inc., out of her bedroom. She was going to be a professional fiduciary. She had been a public fiduciary for the County of Sacramento many years prior. An opportunity arose and, at the pleading of a local attorney (attorneys know how to plead), she started our little company. What fascinated me was the possibility of joining her in a new, evolving industry.

The population is aging. The baby boomers have a significant amount of wealth to use for their care and to pass on to their beneficiaries, if they have any. The divorce rates of years past, the separation of families through geographic distributions, the increase in dementia and Alzheimer's, and the individuality of people, was creating a market demographic in dire need of a professional fiduciary. Who would make medical decisions for someone without children or spouses? Who would manage finances for an elderly person suffering with dementia or other ailment with no family nearby? Who would protect the vulnerable when children were fighting over money or property? Who would protect the elderly from scam artists and cons?

The professional fiduciary.

I left my career at the surprise of many and joined my wife in 2001. We started with a handful of cases and quickly grew into a formidable company, managing more than 100 cases all over the state of Oregon and beyond. We assisted our state association with the formation of the Public Guardian office of the State of Oregon. We supported our association with drafting legislation defining a professional fiduciary and requiring them to be certified and competent. We have trained other fiduciaries, helped thousands of people, provided expert witness testimony, put criminals in prison, sold mobile home parks, created subdivision, hired many people for and through our company, and sat with many of our clients holding their hand as they took their last breath on this earth.

And it all started with an idea and desire to participate in something new.

This book is intended to share our experience, thoughts, ideas, and concerns about being a professional fiduciary in a way that _anyone_ can understand. If you are entering the fiduciary field as a relative, friend, or for your own estate plan, you need a book like this to explain the basics of each fiduciary role and how to execute it well. The terminology can be daunting; the process overwhelming; the fiduciary's role complicated. You are entering a field of trust. You should know what is expected of you and how to execute your responsibilities. This book will help.

As for me and my career change, I leave you with this quote from Theodore Roosevelt from which I have lived my life:

"Tis far better to dare mighty things, though checkered with failure, than to live in the gray twilight that knows not victory nor defeat."

Jerry Rainey

Chapter One
What is a Fiduciary?

Defining a fiduciary is pretty easy if you just take the definition out of any dictionary or Wikipedia;

Fiduciary – (fi-doo-shee-er-ee) A person to whom property or power is entrusted for the benefit of another.

One often in a position of authority who obligates himself or herself to act on behalf of another (as in managing money or property) and assumes a duty to act in good faith and with care, candor, and <u>loyalty</u> in fulfilling the obligation :one (as an agent) having a fiduciary duty to another.

The word, fiduciary, comes from the Latin *fiduciarius*, from *fiducia* trust, or transfer of a property on trust. Its origin dates back thousands of years. In ancient Roman times, a person was able to transfer their interest in property to another person who would manage or care for it on their behalf. If a person transferred his property to another, on condition that it should be restored to him, this contract was called Fiducia. A person might transfer his property to another for the sake of greater security in time of danger, or for other sufficient reason.

In the Jewish writings, the concept of stewardship is well represented in the earliest writings of the bible. In Genesis, 43, Joseph has several directions for his steward to take care of his affairs. The person was to act as though he was the master. A steward is defined as a person who manages another's property or financial affairs; one who administers anything as the agent of another or others. It wasn't a contract as with the Romans, but an expectation and assignment of trust.

We can see that the concept of taking care or managing the affairs of another person, particularly of a financial appointment, was practiced in ancient times. It was expected that the fiduciary would exercise great scrutiny and self-control to insure that the only interests that were considered were those of the principal, or the person who appointed them. The fiduciary was expected to avoid conflicts of interest, which is where actions taken by them would benefit themselves and not the principal. They must insure every action was for the benefit of the principal. The fiduciary must exercise a high degree of ethical control.

In a situation where a vulnerable person appoints a fiduciary or has a fiduciary appointed on their behalf, a relationship of trust and confidence is created whereby the fiduciary acts _solely_ on behalf of the principal. A fiduciary duty is one that requires the highest standard of care and ethics. A fiduciary is expected to be extremely loyal to the person to whom he owes the duty (the "principal"): such that there must be no conflict of duty between fiduciary and principal, and the fiduciary must not profit from his position as a fiduciary, unless the principal consents.

The fiduciary has a duty not to be in a situation where personal interests and fiduciary duty conflict, not to be in a situation where his fiduciary duty conflicts with another fiduciary duty, and a duty not to profit from his fiduciary position without knowledge and consent. A fiduciary ideally would not have a conflict of interest, which we will explain more about later in this book. A fiduciary is expected to operate at a level higher than expected from a common person, and with greater integrity and ethics than the common man. _They should exercise undivided loyalty to the principal, even above their own interests_.

It is a great responsibility to become a fiduciary for another.

The definitions and expectations of fiduciaries are well explained in the laws of the jurisdiction of appointment. Each state has laws or statutes that define the obligations, expectations, limitations and requirements of fiduciary appointments. State laws can vary in any of the above areas, but, generally speaking, the intent of the fiduciary appointment and obligations are very similar; **_the interests of the principal comes first_**.

Layman as Fiduciary

There are professional fiduciaries and laymen acting as fiduciaries. Professionals are neutral, third parties who are paid to execute the role as a fiduciary. I'll cover more on that later. The layman is the mom and pop, son, daughter, other relative or friend who want to step in and help a person in need.

During everyone's life, there is a high probability that a time will come where a fiduciary is needed. It may be creating an estate plan, such as a trust or will, or making sure someone can make medical decisions on their behalf. It can be the result of careful planning, which is always preferred, or a crisis event.

Several years ago I was working on the roof of our recreational vehicle and fell off an eight foot ladder. I landed on my head and shoulders on the asphalt and was nearly knocked unconscious. I was fortunate that I was not killed or crippled from the fall. Had I been, a fiduciary would have been needed to either manage my medical needs or settle my estate.

Many people suffer cognitive decline as they age. This is called dementia. It usually manifests itself in diminished reasoning abilities, memory loss, or confusion. The most aggressive form is Alzheimer's; a dreaded and horrible disease.

We are vulnerable to many catalysts that can require a fiduciary be appointed over our persons or estate. The remainder of this book will define the fiduciary roles that can be exercised by a layman or professional fiduciary.

Professional Fiduciary

There are instances where a layman, such as a family member or friend, may not be the best solution to fill a fiduciary need. Adult children could be arguing over the best care for their parent, or the settlement of an estate. Or, maybe the person has no family or friends to step in and help. That is when a professional fiduciary could be the right solution.

A professional fiduciary is one who operates as a fiduciary specifically as a business or profession. Each state might have a definition of what constitutes a professional fiduciary. Be sure to review your state laws and understand what constitutes a professional fiduciary. In Oregon, a professional fiduciary is a person nominated as a fiduciary or serving as a fiduciary who is acting at the same time as a fiduciary for three or more persons who are not related to the fiduciary.

When a professional fiduciary is appointed, often there are much higher standards and scrutiny that are met before the appointment. _The petition and requirements are much more detailed than if a family member was to be appointed._ In Oregon, the petition for the appointment of a professional fiduciary contains the following information;

- Proof that the professional fiduciary, or an individual responsible for making decisions for clients or for managing client assets for the professional fiduciary, is certified by the Center for Guardianship Certification or its successor organization as a National Certified Guardian or a National Master Guardian.
- A description of the events that led to the involvement of the professional fiduciary in the case.
- The educational background, professional experience, investment credentials and licensing of the individual responsible as, or acting on behalf of, the professional fiduciary.
- The fees charged by the professional fiduciary and whether the fees are on an hourly basis or are based on charges for individual services rendered, including whether there is any revenue sharing arrangement between the professional fiduciary and any other person.
- The method by which the fees will be assessed or charged, whether by commissions, monthly charges or any other method.
- The names of providers of direct services to protected persons that are repeatedly used by the professional fiduciary under contract.
- If the person nominated to act as a professional fiduciary will employ a person in which the nominated person has a pecuniary or financial interest, that relationship must be fully disclosed.

- The number of protected persons for whom the person performs fiduciary services at the time of the petition.
- Whether the professional fiduciary has ever had a claim against the bond[1] of the professional fiduciary and a description of the circumstances causing the claim.
- Whether the professional fiduciary or any staff with responsibility for making decisions for clients or for management of client assets has ever filed for bankruptcy and the date of filing.
- Whether the professional fiduciary or any staff with responsibility for making decisions for clients or for management of client assets has ever been denied a professional license that is directly related to responsibilities of the professional fiduciary, or has ever held a professional license that is directly related to responsibilities of the professional fiduciary that was revoked or canceled. If such a license has been denied, revoked or canceled, the petition must reflect the date of the denial, revocation or cancellation and the name of the regulatory body that denied, revoked or canceled the license.
- A statement that the criminal records check does not disqualify the person from acting as a professional fiduciary.
- Whether the professional fiduciary and any staff responsible for making decisions for clients or for management of client assets is or has been certified by a national or state association of professional fiduciaries, the name of any such association and whether the professional fiduciary or other staff person has ever been disciplined by any such association and the result of the disciplinary action.
- The name, address and telephone number of the individual who is to act as primary decision maker for the protected person and the name of the person with whom the protected person will have personal contact if that person is not the person who will act as primary decision maker for the protected person.
- An acknowledgment by the professional fiduciary that the professional fiduciary will make all investments of client assets in accordance with the standards set forth in Oregon law.

---

[1] **Bond** – Insurance for a specific purpose, such as mismanagement by a fiduciary resulting in a loss to the estate.

- If a petition seeks the appointment of a professional fiduciary, the professional fiduciary and all staff with responsibility for making decisions for clients or for management of client assets must undergo a criminal records check before the court may appoint the professional fiduciary. The results of the criminal records check shall be provided by the petitioner to the court. Results of criminal records checks submitted to the court are confidential, shall be subject to inspection only by the parties to the proceedings and their attorneys, and shall not be subject to inspection by members of the public except pursuant to a court order entered after a showing of good cause. A professional fiduciary must disclose to the court any criminal conviction of the professional fiduciary that occurs after the criminal records check was performed. The criminal records check under this subsection shall consist of a check for a criminal record in the State of Oregon and a national criminal records check if:
  - The person has resided in another state within five years before the date that the criminal records check is performed;
  - The person has disclosed the existence of a criminal conviction; or
  - A criminal records check in Oregon discloses the existence of a criminal record in another jurisdiction.

You can see that the court requires a lot of information and scrutinizes the appropriateness of appointing a professional fiduciary. It is important that a professional fiduciary insures they have the physical capacity to manage the case they are to be appointed on and not be stretched too thin. The professional fiduciary must be diligent with each case, thorough with each case, and fully understand the nature of each case. The professional fiduciary cannot be so overwhelmed that a case becomes a burden and they are unable to effectively manage it because of the size of their caseload. If that occurs, then every case they manage is at risk.

You can see that the requirements for a professional fiduciary are significant. The requirements for a relative as a fiduciary are much less stringent. The courts always prefer to have a relative or friend be a fiduciary instead of a professional if the appointment is appropriate.

Types of fiduciary relationships

There are a variety of fiduciary appointments that require a relationship of trust between parties. Each of these appointments and relationships will be defined in detail later in this book.

- Trustee and beneficiaries
- Conservatorship and the protected person or ward[2]
- Guardianship and the protected person or ward
- Power of Attorney (Agent) and the Principal
- Personal Representatives or Executors and heirs

Other arrangements of fiduciaries and other parties are;

- Doctor and patient
- Lawyer and client
- Priest and parishioner
- Banks and depositors
- Retirement Plan Administrators and beneficiaries
- Investment advisors and investors
- Real estate broker and client
- Teacher and student

There are other relationships of a fiduciary nature not covered in either of the lists above. You can see that each of these appointments require an element of trust and loyalty. For purposes of this writing, we will focus on the first list in the remainder of this book.

Conflicts of interest

A fiduciary is said to have a conflict of interest when the interest of the fiduciary conflicts with the interest of the principal, such that the decision making of the fiduciary is corrupted. A conflict of interest exists if the

---

[2] **Ward** – A person under guardianship or conservatorship and oversight by the court.

circumstances are reasonably believed (on the basis of past experience and objective evidence) to create a risk that a decision _may_ be unduly influenced by other, secondary interests, and not on whether a particular individual is actually influenced by a secondary interest. A conflict of interest can occur with a layman fiduciary or a professional fiduciary.

For example; a fiduciary may decide to sell their personal car to a principal. Even if the car was sold below market value, it could easily be perceived that a conflict of interest has occurred because the interests of the fiduciary could have been corrupted by the willingness to sell the car to the principal. Maybe the car has problems that were not disclosed. Maybe the fiduciary wanted to sell the car and take advantage of a better deal on a different car. Whatever the reasons, it does not matter. The conflict occurs **_when it is perceived_** that the fiduciary may profit or benefit from the activity above the interest of the principal. There may not be an actual conflict, but the perception of one is sufficient to create the conflict.

Another example might be when a fiduciary hires a family member to provide services to a principal; say a son is fiduciary and he hires his son (or grandson to the principal) to clean the yards. Even if the services by a family member could be obtained at a lower cost, the conflict of interest occurs when it is _perceived_ that the fiduciary or family member would benefit from the arrangement.

It is imperative that every action of the fiduciary is weighed against potential conflicts of interest, and either avoided or disclosed to the proper channels to assure the interests of the principal are first and foremost in the decision. We will go into more detail near the end of the book regarding conflicts of interest.

Retain/Employ Professionals

Most fiduciary appointments authorize the fiduciary to retain or employ professionals. This is a broad authorization that should be utilized. When you are appointed as a fiduciary, you could be thrust into a position of making decisions that are beyond your education, experience, or knowledge. Often, estates have multiple properties to manage. Unique assets could be discovered or be a part of the estate.

Case Study - I was appointed as trustee of a large estate that had acreage and a plan to develop the property into a subdivision. The prior trustee had plans to do it his way, resulting in conflicts amongst the beneficiaries and my subsequent appointment as a neutral third party. I had no idea of how to develop a piece of property into a subdivision, but over the next year and with many meetings with land use planners, surveyors, the County Planning Commission, contractors, and beneficiaries of the trust, I developed a plan to create the subdivision and double the value of the trust. If I had moved forward based on my knowledge, I could have sold the property as is and lost value for the beneficiaries.

As a fiduciary of a person, you could encounter rare diseases, or ailments that could be contracted by your ward and you could be required to oversee the care and administration of treatment. It would be imperative that you consult with as many professionals as possible to assure you understand the diagnosis, prognosis and treatment for an individual.

As a fiduciary, you will have the authority to employ professionals to assist you with managing a case. My suggestion; ***use it***.

Neutral Third Party

A professional fiduciary is seldom appointed in a simple, easy-to-mange, "everyone-gets-along" type of case. Far from it. A professional fiduciary is usually appointed in a contentious, difficult, dangerous case where either all of the parties are arguing, someone is being abused, or some situation has occurred where no one is able or willing to deal with it. It's nice when someone just wants to name a professional in their estate plan because they have no one else, and the plan is simple, but that rarely happens.

Just to give you an idea of what a professional fiduciary may have to deal with, the following are some actual cases that we have had over the years;

- Brothers chasing each other with guns.
- A husband murdered his wife with the help of one of his sons. The surviving son needed a conservator, and the deceased wife needed a personal representative to close her estate.
- A woman who would take her prosthetic leg off and beat people on a bus, go to jail, go to the hospital, be discharged to the street, and repeat the cycle over and over and over again.
- Children arguing over a parent's estate, and accusing each other of either abuse or theft.
- A policeman who took hundreds of thousands of dollars from his parent's estate.
- A power of attorney who stole more than $400,000 from an elderly woman in eighteen months.
- An estate that needed a personal representative to remove sixteen meth addicts from the property and sell the property to a developer.
- A grandmother who was in the middle of a raid on her home that included the Alcohol, Tobacco and Firearms (ATF), Sheriff SWAT team, local police and National Guard assault vehicle to blow a hole in the wall and gain access to take down her grandson.
- A woman who hoarded so much that her apartment was so full she had to sleep in the front doorway ------ ***standing up***.

And on, and on, and on.

These are not simple cases, and managing them and distributing them is not always a simple task. One thing that is common in each and every case for a professional fiduciary is:

- Remain neutral
- Work solely for the benefit of the protected person, ward, beneficiary[3] or estate
- Use professionals to help you manage the case and work through the process

---

[3] **Beneficiary** - A person who derives advantage from something, especially a trust, will, or life insurance policy.

The more neutral you remain as a professional or layman fiduciary, the more non-confrontational you can be, the more professional you are, the better the case will go. Even with all of these difficult cases over the years, we have only had one case where we were directly threatened. We petitioned the court, with the agreement of the remainder beneficiaries, to be removed from the case and distribute the assets of the trust prematurely to the threatening party, rather than try and manage the trust as directed by the trustors.

Co-Fiduciaries

Almost any fiduciary appointment can be done with a co-fiduciary. That means that two people work in unison to manage a case. There can be co-conservators, co-trustees and co-guardians. Occasionally, a family member will ask to be co-fiduciary with another family member. We believe it is best **_not_** to be appointed as co-fiduciary with any family member. Each family member likely have a lot of history and will make decisions based more on emotion or history than facts or best interests of the protected person. This will create immediate conflict between the fiduciaries.

The co-fiduciary can also unwind or obstruct the other fiduciary's actions. This can easily result in petitions to the court for instructions, raising the expenses of managing the case and creating friction between the fiduciaries.

Our opinion is that it is better to act as a sole fiduciary.

Considerations for the Fiduciary

A fiduciary has a significant duty and responsibility to the principal or estate. It is imperative that the fiduciary review the proposed appointment to assure they understand the requirements of their appointment and that they have the ability and resources to effectively manage the appointment. _Do your homework before you get appointed._

Chapter 2
Power of Attorney

One of the most basic of fiduciary appointments is the Power of Attorney.

A power of attorney (POA) is a written authorization to have a person represent or act on another's behalf in private affairs, business, or some other legal matter. The person authorizing the other to act is the principal, grantor, or donor (of the power). The one authorized to act is the agent or the attorney-in-fact. The agent must make decisions and take actions that _only_ benefit the principal as if the principal had made the decision.

The appointment of an agent as power of attorney does not restrict the principal from continuing to act on their own behalf. This can create an environment where the principal and the agent take conflicting actions, or duplicate actions, or can cause funds to be mismanaged because of duplication of effort or poor communication. An agent must be in communication with the principal and act on behalf of the principal to avoid such dilemmas.

The principal who creates the power of attorney must have the capacity to do so. Capacity is often determined by an attorney at the time the document is executed. The difficulty in today's world of immediate access to online documents is that capacity of a principal is seldom reviewed by anyone, much less someone of competence as an attorney. This can cause the validity of such an executed power of attorney to be suspect.

A power of attorney does not need to be notarized or witnessed in many states. Each state has their laws regarding the creation and execution of a power of attorney. It is imperative to know the laws of the state before someone executes such a document. Even if a state has no requirements of notarizing or witnessing the execution of a power of attorney, it would be prudent for the principal to request such oversight. However, often a person is in a state of confusion, distress, or chaos and attempts to correct the situation through the easiest means available; a power of attorney, with no thought of the legal requirements or implications of delegating such authority.

For example, a person who has no children may decide to have a friend become POA if they become sick or miss some payments of importance, such as utility payments. Rather than admit they are struggling, they could be convinced, or even coerced, into appointing another person without legal counsel. Such actions set the stage for financial abuse, contesting decisions and actions, or added confusion if multiple powers of attorney exist.

Case Study – I was approached by Adult Protective Services (APS) regarding a case where they were contacted by a credit union with concerns about one of their members; an elderly woman. They noticed tens of thousands of dollars had been withdrawn by the power of attorney for the woman over the past year.

I met with APS and the elderly woman, Jane, to discuss the situation. I discovered Jane's husband recently passed away and Jane sold their house and moved into a manufactured home. She volunteered at the soup kitchen at the mission and befriended a woman there twenty years her junior. The woman, Anna, became good friends with Jane and moved in with her after only knowing her for six months.

Anna helped a lot around the house; cleaning, cooking, and getting mail. After a short period, Jane complained about not being able to stay up on her finances. It was becoming too confusing. Jane had some moderate dementia and was forgetting things. Anna offered to help her pay bills by writing the checks and Jane could sign them. They agreed and Anna helped her for several months.

As time progressed, Anna brought up to Jane that it would be better if she could be power of attorney because then she could contact the credit union if she had any problems balancing the checkbook. Jane agreed and made her POA.

Over the next eighteen months, Anna took more than $400,000 from Jane's investment accounts. Anna fled to Texas and Jane was nearly broke. I *contacted the local police and agreed to put a case together with them, for free, and help prosecute Anna. I gathered the financial information and entered it into Quickbooks to analyze the data. What I discovered was that most of the ATM transactions occurred in New Mexico at a particular casino. The police were able to obtain a warrant for the New Mexico gaming commission to obtain gamboling records from the casino on the perpetrator. We discovered Anna gamboled more than $232,000 at one casino----using her player's club card!*

After a year and many hours of volunteer time, including me testifying before the grand jury, Anna was charged with elder abuse and extradited from Texas. She pled guilty and was sentenced to five years in prison.

Jane never got her money back because Anna gambled it away. Jane's daughter became her power of attorney and is helping her mother with the few remaining assets of her estate.

A power of attorney is a serious document that grants broad authority and can easily be misused. Jane granted significant authority to a person she hardly knew while she was lonely and vulnerable and suffering from mild cognitive impairment. Jane could have authorized a limited power of attorney, or other type, to minimize the person's authority. Jane should have gone to an attorney to have the right type of power of attorney drafted and make sure she had capacity to execute one.

There are several types of powers of attorney.

General Financial POA

A general financial power of attorney is one where a principal appoints an agent to act on their behalf regarding all financial affairs. Some of the areas of authority are:

- Real estate transactions – buy, sell, rent, lease, dispose, acquire, mortgage, develop properties, etc.

- Tangible personal property transactions – buy, sell, trade, modify, dispose, lease, etc.

- Bond, share and commodity transactions – buy, sell, leverage, etc.

- Banking transactions – open, close accounts at any financial institution, accept deposits, write checks, accept retirement funds, social security, pensions, federal pensions, Medicaid and Medicare qualifications, investments of all types, precious metals, access to safe deposit boxes, etc.

- Business operating transactions – buy, sell, encumber a business, perform all activities of a business operation, hire, terminate employees, sell shares, obtain loans, etc.

- Insurance transactions – purchase, liquidate insurances, annuities, designate beneficiaries, etc.

- Gifts to charities and individuals other than Attorney-in-Fact.

- Claims and litigation – represent the principal in any and all claims and litigation. Accept mediation, pursue litigation, hire attorneys, etc.

- Benefits from military service – accept, apply for, process claims and benefits for military service or government employment, etc.

- Records, reports and statements – receive, process, destroy, manage, copy, distribute any and all records or statements of the principal, etc.

- Full and unqualified authority to the attorney-in-fact to delegate any or all of the foregoing powers to any persons whom the attorney-in-fact shall select.

- All other matters written by the principal.

You can see that a general power of attorney grants tremendous authority and power to an individual to act on behalf of the principal.

A general financial power of attorney continues until the principal becomes incapacitated or dies. The POA authority terminates at that time, and the agent could be liable for any actions they take after such an event. Incapacity is typically determined by a medical practitioner, such as a doctor, psychiatrist, etc. The principal can also terminate the POA at any time.

Durable POA

A durable power of attorney is one that becomes effective, or remains in effect, when the principal becomes incapacitated and continues until the death of the principal. The durable power of attorney can contain all of the same elements of a general financial power of attorney. The primary difference is the issue of incapacity and the effect that has on the authority of the agent.

Limited POA

A limited power of attorney, or sometimes called a special power of attorney, is one that delegates a specific authority to an agent from a principal.

Case Study – A person could be traveling the world and not have immediate access to fax machines, scanners, or other devices that would enable them to execute documents. If that person was a part of a large litigation case, their original signature might be critical for the continuation of the case. The person could appoint an agent under a limited power of attorney to sign documents approved by the principal on behalf of the principal. That way, the principal could continue to travel to remote places, review documents online, and forward the approved documents to the agent to execute under the limited power of attorney on their behalf with instructions on where to mail the executed documents. This may sound far-fetched, but I have personally been appointed in such a capacity. The principal was elated that we could develop such a relationship and enable them to continue to travel the world without fear of missing a document or deadline needed for the litigation.

Another example might be for a principal to appoint an agent to sell or transfer specific property, such as a vehicle. Most limited powers of attorney are similar to this, in that they authorize an agent to execute some limited transaction as directed by the principal.

Temporary POA

A temporary power of attorney is just that; it is an appointment of an agent by a principal for a specific duration. The power of attorney expires at the end of the appointed time.

Springing POA

Occasionally, a person may need a power of attorney appointed if a situation occurs. A springing power of attorney is one that becomes effective when an action or situation occurs. For example, a principal may create a power of attorney to begin, or spring, when they are incarcerated. The agent gains their authority at the time of the event, which should be well documented. It can be limited in duration.

Healthcare POA

A healthcare power of attorney is one where a principal appoints an agent to act on their behalf regarding any and all medical decisions. This is a significant appointment. Under a healthcare power of attorney, the agent can make decisions and take such actions regarding;

- The power to direct the withholding or withdrawal of life-prolonging treatment, including artificially supplied nutrition and hydration/tube feeding;
- Consent, refuse, or withdraw consent to any care, procedure, treatment, or service to diagnose, treat, or maintain a physical or mental condition, including artificial nutrition and hydration;
- Permit, refuse, or withdraw permission to participate in federally regulated research related to the principal's condition or disorder;
- Make all necessary arrangements for any hospital, psychiatric treatment facility, hospice, nursing home, or other healthcare organization; and, employ or discharge healthcare personnel (any person who is authorized or permitted by the laws of the state to provide healthcare services) as he or she shall deem necessary for the principal's physical, mental, or emotional well-being;

- Request, receive, review, and authorize sending any information regarding the principal's physical or mental health, or personal affairs, including medical and hospital records; and execute any releases that may be required to obtain such information;
- Move the principal into or out of any State or institution;
- Take legal action, if needed;
- Make decisions about autopsy, tissue and organ donation, and the disposition of the principal's body in conformity with state law;
- Become the principal's guardian if one is needed.

This is an appointment where the principal literally turns their life over to the agent. Often a healthcare power of attorney will revoke any and all durable powers of attorney that may include healthcare provisions. It is important that a healthcare power of attorney be created by a competent principal with great thought and consideration for the implications of the appointment. The principal and agent should also discuss at length the wishes of the principal. Often a healthcare power of attorney is appointed within the development of the advanced directives of the principal, which we cover in detail later in this book.

Considerations for the Fiduciary

Becoming the agent under a power of attorney has inherent risks for the fiduciary. I know some professional fiduciaries who will never accept an agent appointment under a power of attorney. They prefer to be appointed conservator (which we will cover in more detail later) or have a trust created and appoint them as trustee. Powers of attorney are too prevalent, and the capacity of the principal can go unquestioned. That opens the fiduciary to unnecessary scrutiny should a problem arise.

For a family member or layman, a power of attorney could be an excellent, less expensive solution to manage a loved one's finances and affairs. If you happen to accept an appointment as an agent, be sure to fully understand the authority being granted to you. Read every line of the document and if questions arise, ask an attorney. Hopefully, the principal has an attorney that drafted the document. If the power of attorney is 'off the shelf,' be it a store or online download, avoid it. Those seldom are specific to the state of execution and could be fraught with errors or conflicts. Ask the principal to execute a power of attorney with an attorney and, hopefully, one drafted by an attorney. That would provide measurably more protection for the fiduciary and the principal. The capacity of the principal would be assessed by the attorney, the document would be specific for the state of execution, and you would be assured most of your bases are covered for you as the agent. If not, you can go to the attorney for the principal for clarification.

Another issue that I covered earlier is the possibility of duplication or neglect of actions. Be sure you have a thorough discussion with the principal to understand who will be responsible for what. You, as a fiduciary, do not need to have a situation where you are the agent on a power of attorney and write a series of checks that bounce because the principal went into the financial institution and withdrew several thousand dollars.....and gave it away. Not only will you have to explain why you overdrew the account, but you could be called to account for not protecting the account better for the principal, especially if they show any signs of dementia or diminished capacity, even long after the appointment.

Sometimes the principal has agreed to pay the layman fiduciary for services. As with any appointment, be sure to have an agreement in place between you and the principal for payment for your services. The power of attorney may indicate an agent may be entitled to fair compensation, but what is fair? It is always best to be clear about your fees and expectations for payment through an agreement and disclosure between parties.

A final consideration is that your authority can be revoked at any time. You could be writing checks after the principal contacted the financial institution that your power of attorney has been revoked and replaced. You could find yourself writing checks without authority, or attempting to withdraw funds without authority.

To summarize, tread cautiously when considering being appointed as an agent under a power of attorney. Make certain the document is well drafted, properly executed, that the principal has capacity, that the authorities are clear, and that your fees for services are well disclosed. Anything short of that is asking for trouble.

Chapter 3
Trusts and Trustees

Many people create a trust to manage their estates. So, what is a trust?

A trust is a fiduciary relationship in which one party, known as a trustor, gives another party, the trustee (person managing the trust), the right to hold title to property or assets for the benefit of a third party, the beneficiary. Often, the trustor, trustee, and beneficiary are all the same person. Trusts are established to provide legal protection for the trustor's assets, to make sure those assets are distributed according to the wishes of the trustor, and to save time, reduce paperwork and, in some cases, avoid or reduce inheritance or estate taxes.

A trust can be a very complicated document. There are many types of trusts, of which this book does not have the time or space to cover. Suffice to say, anyone being appointed as a trustee of a trust _must_ read the trust in its entirety to understand what is expected of them to execute the terms of the trust per the wishes of the trustor.

Trustor/Grantor/Settlor/Donor

The person who establishes the trust is known as the trustor, grantor, settlor or donor. The titles are pretty much interchangeable, depending upon jurisdiction. The trustor will typically meet with an estate planning attorney and create the trust as part of their estate plan.

Objective of the Trust

The objective of the trust is defined at the beginning of the trust. There are so many types of trusts that we will not go into great detail here. Most trusts in estate planning focus on establishing the trust by the trustor, managed by the trustee who is often the same person as the trustor, for the benefit of the beneficiary, who, again, is the trustor. Some trusts are established for the benefit of a third party. Trusts can also create secondary trusts for a third party beneficiary. Trusts can be for people, pets, or other entities. The flexibility of a trust document is what can make it so difficult to manage.

Case Study - I was asked to be trustee of a trust that allowed for regular distributions to an adult child if they were 'drug free and not dependent upon alcohol or drugs.' That may sound simple, but what drugs would be considered that the beneficiary needed to be 'drug free' from? Would that include aspirin? Antibiotics? How would I test? How often? How would I know if the beneficiary used alcohol or was alcohol dependent? You can see that executing the terms of the trust as defined would be virtually impossible.

The objective of most trusts is to provide for the beneficiary, who often is the trustor, until death, at which time the trust assets would be distributed as the trust directs.

Several Kinds of Trust

Trusts come in all shapes and sizes. There are many types of trusts, but for this book we will focus on four; revocable living trust, irrevocable trust, supplemental or special needs trust and income cap trusts.

Revocable Trust (Living Trust)
Revocable trusts are created during the lifetime of the trustor and can be altered, changed, modified or revoked entirely. Often called a living trust, these are trusts in which the trustor transfers the title of a property to a trust, serves as the initial trustee, and has the ability to remove the property from the trust during his or her lifetime. Typically, a revocable trust evolves into an irrevocable trust upon the death of the trustor. Revocable trusts can be modified, or amended, at any time.

Irrevocable Trust
An irrevocable trust is one which cannot be altered, changed, modified or revoked after its creation. Once a property is transferred to an irrevocable trust, no one, including the trustor, can take the property out of the trust. Often, a revocable trust can become irrevocable if the trust rules identify a situation that would cause it to become irrevocable, such as the incapacity of the trustor.

Special Needs Trust (Supplemental Needs Trust)
A special needs trust (also known as a supplemental needs trust) is one which is created for a person who receives government benefits so as not to disqualify the beneficiary from such government benefits. This is completely legal and permitted under the Social Security rules provided that the disabled beneficiary cannot control the amount or the frequency of trust distributions and cannot revoke the trust. The beneficiary may not receive cash from the trust. The trust also cannot purchase food or shelter for the beneficiary. The intent of the trust is to provide for the supplement needs of the beneficiary; not the basic life needs such as food and shelter, which are provided by Medicaid or other government benefits. Each state has their own rules regarding Medicaid qualifications and benefits and the use of these trusts. Not following the rules of the trust could cause the beneficiary to lose government benefits through disqualification.

Ordinarily when a person is receiving government benefits, an inheritance or receipt of a gift could reduce or eliminate the person's eligibility for such benefits. The trustor creates their estate plan with the intent to transfer their estate into a special needs trust at the time of death to protect the government benefits of the beneficiary of the estate.

By establishing a trust, which provides supplemental needs of the disabled person which otherwise could not be obtained by the beneficiary, the beneficiary can obtain the benefits from the trust without defeating his or her eligibility for government benefits. Usually, a special needs trust has a provision which terminates the trust in the event that it could be used to make the beneficiary ineligible for government benefits.

Supplemental or special needs has a specific legal definition and is defined as the requisites for maintaining the comfort and happiness of a disabled person, when such requisites are not being provided by any public or private agency. These needs can include

- medical and dental expenses not covered by Medicaid
- medical equipment not covered by Medicaid
- education

- treatment
- rehabilitation
- eye glasses
- transportation (including vehicle purchase)
- maintenance
- insurance (including payment of premiums of insurance on the life of the beneficiary)
- essential dietary needs
- electronic and computer equipment
- vacations
- athletic contests
- movies
- travel
- payments for a companion
- socialization (meals out)
- Entertainment
- and other items to enhance self-esteem.

The list is quite extensive. Typically, cash, food and shelter are omitted from the list of approved expenditures.

One comment on Socialization. Often, a disabled person may have difficulties going out to events or places and stays in a facility for lengthy periods. Socialization is where a person, like a companion, can take the person out for a meal and the food is covered by the trust. This is the only area where food would be covered by the trust. Direct purchases of food to be consumed in the home are not allowed by the trust.

Parents of a disabled child can establish a special needs trust as part of their general estate plan and not worry that their child will be disqualified from receiving benefits when they are not there to care for the child. Disabled persons who expect an inheritance or other large sum of money may establish a special needs trust themselves, provided that another person or entity is named as trustee. A conservator can create a special needs trust for their ward.

Income Cap Trust

Similar to a special needs trust, an income cap trust is for those beneficiaries receiving government assistance who have more monthly income than the Medicaid limit allows for. The funds go into an income cap trust and are administered by a trustee. For example, if the Medicaid limit for monthly income is $2,300.00, and a person has $4,000 of monthly income but no assets, then an income cap trust would be established to receive all of the beneficiary's income while keeping them qualified for Medicaid. The trust would contain a distribution schedule where all but a small amount would go to housing (facility payment). The remainder is for personal use, such as clothes, toiletries, haircuts, etc. These types of trusts are managed by a third party trustee, who is allowed to take $50.00 per month as income for managing the trust. This amount, and the rules for an income cap trust, can vary from state to state. Be sure to understand the state rules of such trusts before you become a trustee for one. Seldom can anyone manage such a trust for $50.00 at a profit or breakeven. Typically, these are considered 'pro bono' cases (free or no charge) and are often managed by a family member or friend.

Property

The trustor must identify the property to go into the trust. The trustee must transfer that property into the trust. The property can be real property (house, land, etc), personal property (furniture, cars, etc), bank accounts, cash, investments, businesses ventures, etc. It is important to follow through and transfer the property into the trust. If this is not done, then the property is not able to be managed by the trustee.

Often, the trust will have a provision that empowers the trustee to receive any property into the trust that they want to receive. Therefore, property can be added to the trust at any time.

Personal property is extremely difficult for a trustee to manage and be accountable for. When appointed, the trustee should take a complete inventory of all personal property that is being transferred into the trust. Typically, this is the personal property in the home of the trustor/beneficiary. Trying to manage or control the personal property of someone's home is near impossible. We recommend to clients that personal property be excluded from the trust. On occasion, we have petitioned the court to modify the trust and remove the personal property from the trust and the trustee's oversight.

Note on Pour Over Will

Often, when a person creates a trust, they will also create a 'Pour Over Will." A pour over will is a simple document that transfers anything outside of the trust into the trust at the time of death. This is an excellent solution to managing the personal property. The trustee can avoid the time and expense of managing the personal property in the trust and, when the person passes away, the trustee is able to secure the personal property remaining and distribute it according to the terms of the trust.

The pour over will also transfers any assets, such as small bank accounts or items that were neglected to be added to the trust, back into the trust at the time of death for distribution.

Beneficiary

A beneficiary is the party, or parties, who will benefit from the assets of the trust. Often, the beneficiary is the same person as the trustor. With a special needs trust, it could be a child of the trustor. There can be more than one beneficiary of a trust. There can also be a primary beneficiary who benefits from the trust during their lifetime and a remainder beneficiary (ies) who receives the distribution of the trust at the time of death of the primary beneficiary.

The more the beneficiaries, typically the more complicated the trust, particularly when it is distributed at the death of the trustor. It is important that the trustee diligently performs their duties to avoid future litigation by the remainder beneficiaries. A trustee should manage the trust for the primary beneficiary with a keen eye as to how that will affect the future distribution to the remainder beneficiaries.

Trustee

This is the person, or persons, appointed to manage the trust. Normally, the trustor is also the trustee. A successor trustee is usually named in the body of the trust. A successor takes on the responsibilities of managing the trust when the first trustee is unable or unwilling to serve. There could be several levels of successor trustees. A successor trustee might also be appointed when the first beneficiary, often the trustor, becomes incapacitated. Incapacity is normally defined in the body of the trust. I suggest that incapacity be determined by the beneficiary's primary care physician, with a second opinion from a medical practitioner confirming the diagnosis. This may sound like overkill, but the following example may shed light on why this should be followed.

Case Study – I was appointed as successor trustee of a trust that was created by a trustor who named himself as the beneficiary and trustee. The determination of incapacity in the trust was to have two of the three children of the trustor agree that the trustor was incapacitated. They would not need a medical opinion for determination, only a written statement by two of the three children. If the trustor was deemed incapacitated, then one of the children became successor trustee and the trust became irrevocable.

Two of the three children conspired to have dad deemed incapacitated, and one of them took over the trust. Over the course of the next year, property of the trust was depleted and transferred to the two conspiring children. The third child was left in the cold. The only way to resolve this situation was to litigate, which they did, and appoint me as the successor trustee. The trustor chose not to regain his position as trustee. He did not want to investigate the theft and charge his children.

You can see that the determination of incapacity is critical to protect the beneficiary and to properly execute the wishes of the trustor.

Trust Protector

Some trusts allow for a trust protector to oversee the activities of the trustee. The trust protector can, if provided the authority, terminate the trustee and appoint a successor trustee, or can be the successor trustee. If provided for in the trust, a trust protector can

- receive all annual reports of the trust
- conduct audits or reviews, or have audits or reviews conducted for them
- direct some of the actions of the trustee
- limit some of the actions of the trustee
- replace the trustee
- appoint a new trustee

A trust protector can be anyone. Often, it is a friend or family member who has little knowledge of how a trust operates, or what a fiduciary is. It is important that, if a trust protector is provided for in the trust that you are asked to be trustee for, you have a full understanding of your role as trustee, the role of the trust protector, and the expectations of the principal and trust protector of your duties.

Personally, I prefer to _not_ be appointed in a trust that provides for a trust protector. They often do not fully understand the duties of the trustee and create situations that complicate the process, increase the time of the fiduciary and therefore, the expense of executing the trust.

Structure

There are several main bodies of structure that appear in most, if not all, trusts. They contain the following articles;

Name of the Trust - Name of the trust, type of trust, objective of the trust, and revocability of the trust.

Family - Members of the immediate family of the trustors.

Trust Property -Property to be included in the trust.

Additions to the Trust -Provisions for adding property to the trust.

Revocation and Amendments -Authority to revoke or amend the trust by the trustors.

Disposition of Income and Principal During the Lifetime of the Trustor/Beneficiary- Detailed expectations of distribution of principal and income of the trust. This also includes a definition of incapacity, how it is determined, and what occurs if the trustor becomes incapacitated. Often, the trust becomes irrevocable and a successor trustee is appointed.

Payments and Distribution after the Death of Either Trustor/Beneficiary - This section details the expectations of payment and distributions for the benefit of the remaining trustor.

Distribution of Trust Assets after Death of <u>Both</u> Trustors -This often replaces a person's will. The distributions of the trust assets after the death of the last trustor is the equivalent to a will. This is the section that enables most estates to avoid probating[4] an estate. (Refer to the chapter on personal representatives and wills)

Children's Trusts -This section is to create secondary trusts from the primary trust after both trustors are deceased or other qualifying event defined in the trust.

Trustee Provisions -This explains the parameters of the termination or resignation of a trustee and appointing a successor trustee.

Trustee's Duties and Powers -This details all of the powers of the trustee.

Miscellaneous Provisions -This will have various, miscellaneous provisions of the trust, such as required accountings, payment of services to the trustee, etc.

---

[4] **Probate** - The official proving and processing of a will.

Schedule of Assets transferred into the trust -A detailed list of assets that are transferred into the trust.

Amendments - A trustor can amend a trust if provided the authority in the trust to do so. Amendments replace certain sections or elements of the trust. Sometimes an amendment can be a single sentence, or an entire restatement of a trust. There is no limit to the number of amendments that a trust can have. The latest amendment is the effective one.

Case Study – I was appointed as successor trustee of a large trust that had eight beneficiaries. The two trustors were deceased, so my responsibility was to distribute the assets of the trust to the remainder beneficiaries. After several months, and digging through many boxes, I discovered a second trust that was dated after the date of the first trust. The second trust was intended to be a restatement of the first trust. However, it did not have the word "Restatement" in the title of the document, thus creating a new, second trust.

To add to the confusion, the first trust indicated that if any remainder beneficiary passed away before their share was distributed, their share would go to their issues, or children. The second trust stated that if any remainder beneficiary passed away before their share was distributed, their share would go to the other remainder beneficiaries; not their children. The grandchildren were effectively written out of the trust as future beneficiaries of the trust. Not only that, but the second trust was a copy.

This created a huge problem for me as trustee. I had to petition the court for instructions and prove that the intent of the trustor was to execute the second trust as a restatement of the original trust and remove the grandchildren from becoming beneficiaries. The attorney who drafted the second trust provided an affidavit, or statement, to the court confirming the intent of the trustor to restate the original trust. The court agreed and issued an order to modify the trust and remove the grandchildren as beneficiaries. Then, I had to file a claim against the attorney who drafted the restatement of the trust incorrectly. We settled with the attorney to reimburse the trust the expense it took to rectify the situation.

We thought this solved many issues of the trust, but as you read later in this chapter, this resolution created one big problem that I still had to address; timely distribution of the trust assets.

The omission of one word caused most of the heartache with resolving this situation. Make sure you read the trust in its entirety and understand what is expected of you. If any doubts arise, ask your attorney for clarification.

Certification of trust

Once a trust is created, a certification of trust is created to detail the specific elements of the trust in summary format for the benefit of notifying interested parties, such as financial institutions, government agencies, pension providers, beneficiaries, etc. Rather than send the entire trust as notification of the creation of the trust or a trustee appointment, a certification of trust is sent.

Uniform Trust Code – UTC

The Uniform Trust Code is a model of law that has been adopted by several states. It is a model of law that details the creation, oversight, and execution of a trust. The UTC offers great insight into the duties and responsibilities of the trustee.

Trust Companies and Professional Fiduciaries

Many states require a trust company be the fiduciary or trustee. Becoming a trust company is not a simple process, and subjects the professional fiduciary to extreme scrutiny by government agency oversight and audits. Some states provide for professional fiduciaries to become trustees through court appointment. In Oregon, a professional fiduciary who is not a trust company must petition the court for appointment. The court will review the trust appointment and set a bond for the fiduciary even if the trust does not call for a bond to be established. Check your state laws regarding appointments if you are a professional fiduciary or trust company.

A layman can easily be appointed trustee without court approval. All it takes is the trustor to appoint the layman (family member or friend) and viola! Finished. They are now trustee. The trust will indicate if a bond is required or not.

Bond

A bond is insurance to protect the trust from loss due to mismanagement of the trust by the trustee. Most trusts do not call for a bond. If a professional fiduciary must petition the court for appointment as trustee, then a bond may be required.

Considerations for the Fiduciary

The flexibility of a trust creates a document that can be quite complex and difficult to manage. It is imperative that the fiduciary who accepts an appointment as trustee know what is expected of them to manage the trust.

If a trust protector is involved, you might want to reconsider the appointment.

Understand the issue of incapacity. If the determination of incapacity is not clear, or is cumbersome or questionable, talk with the trustor or their attorney to understand how it is implemented.

If personal property is in the trust, as many are, be aware of the complications of managing this asset. Do a thorough inventory and insure the property. Discuss the management of the personal property with the trustor or beneficiary and come to an agreement on how the property should be managed, Document the agreement if necessary through a letter of understanding. Consult with your attorney. If at all possible, petition to have the personal property removed from the trust and the trustee's oversight.

When you are called to distribute the assets of the trust at the time of the beneficiary's death, be sure to understand what the trust is directing and execute it to the best of your ability. Often, trusts, and wills, will state that the assets are to be liquidated and divided evenly amongst the beneficiaries. You should do this in a timely manner. The trust will typically state that, if one of the beneficiaries predeceases the death of the final trustor, then their share of the assets is to go to their children, or heirs. The trust could say that the assets would go to the remaining beneficiaries, who could be siblings, charities, or other persons and _not_ the heirs of the original beneficiary. Any delay with settling the trust could result in serious accusations toward the trustee of depriving an heir.

Case Study - (continued) – The trust that we restated that I was appointed trustee of had acreage positioned to be developed into a subdivision. It takes a great deal of time to go through a process to create a subdivision and sell lots. The beneficiaries of the trust were the eight siblings stated above. The trust specified that the beneficiaries were to receive the trust assets evenly and, if one beneficiary predeceased distribution of the trust assets, their share would go to the remaining beneficiaries and not their heirs (after we petitioned the court to accept the restatement of trust). In essence, all of the grandchildren were omitted from ever becoming a beneficiary of the trust. If I distributed the assets of the trust immediately, the grandchildren would stand to receive their inheritance if their parent passed away. If I delayed, they would not, giving way for a possible claim against me for breach of fiduciary duty by not distributing the assets of the trust in a timely manner. I either I had to distribute the assets right away, and not get the full value for developing the subdivision for the beneficiaries and face possible claims, or delay and have a beneficiary pass away before I settle the trust, and face possible claims from their children. I was in a no win situation.

Or so I thought.

I met with the beneficiaries and proposed two options; I could distribute the property to them each with a fractional interest in the land. Then they would have to create the subdivision together and sell the lots. This was not ideal because their disagreements before led to my appointment. How could they possibly reach an agreement on a price for a sale with eight differing opinions of value? Titling the properties into the names of the eight beneficiaries would protect their heirs, but the feasibility of this working was not good.

The second option was to create a Limited Liability Company (LLC) with the eight beneficiaries as equal owners of the company. Then, I would distribute the trust property to the LLC and have the LLC continue with the creation and sale of the subdivision. This way, each owner of the LLC could designate in their estate plan what they wanted to do with their shares of the LLC if they pass away before the creation and sale of the subdivision lots.

The siblings liked the idea and agreed to it as long as I was the LLC manager. We continued with our plan to create the LLC, transfer the assets of the trust to the LLC, close the trust, created a contract with my company and the LLC for me to be manager and continue with the development of the subdivision. We turned a 'no-win' situation into a 'win-win' for all of us.

Here is another consideration in dealing with the distribution of personal property of the trust; sometimes, the trust will devise (designate) certain pieces of personal property to certain individuals, like a painting to a niece, silverware to a child, and so on. These requests are pretty easy to execute if you have the property at the time of your appointment. The difficulties surface when the trust states to divide the property evenly, or that the beneficiaries can chose what they want and agree to it. This can be an unmanageable request if any of the beneficiaries are arguing.

What we do in most cases is hire an estate sale company to sell the personal property of the estate. The estate sale company will come in after we have inventoried and searched the assets and prepare the personal property for the estate sale. The estate sales companies we use will normally charge 30-40% to conduct the sale. They will go through every item, price it, remove all pictures and personal items (anything with a name on it, documents, trophies, etc), and prepare for a sale. Then, we offer the family members to come to the sale for a preview. If they are arguing, then let one person at a time preview the items. They are allowed to select anything they want. The estate sale company will tag it (or list it) and run a total. If two persons want the same thing, we put their names in a bowl and draw for a winner. The total of all of their selected items becomes a part of their distributive share. We have done this on many, many cases successfully. The key here is to detail the process, get them to agree, and control the process. This also works well for conservatorships, small estates or probates.

Case Study – We were appointed as conservator on an estate and had an estate sale company come in and prepare the items for sale. We went through the assets and thought we had conducted a pretty detailed search. The family was out of state so there was no preview. The estate sale was conducted and the assets sold.

We made two mistakes during this process. First, we chose an estate sale company that we had not worked with before and had no references with professional fiduciaries that we could check. They had been in the business a long time in their area. It was in a different county than we normally operate in. We tried them out for the first time.

The second mistake was, because it was in a different county and we had family members out of state and not able to preview the items, we did not search through the estate sale items ourselves a second time just before the sale. The estate sale company conducted the sale and gave us a poor list (inventory) of items that were sold.

About a month later, I received a phone call from a nephew of the protected person who was a rabid football fan of a particular college. He said his uncle's championship watch was up for sale on EBAY. I researched the situation and discovered one of the items sold at the estate sale was a watch of the protected person who was one of the coaches for a football team who won a national championship. Each coach received a beautiful watch as a token of their participation in the winning season. The coach's name was inscribed on the back of the watch in full view on EBAY. I tried to win the watch, but was significantly outbid. I contacted the buyer and explained the situation. He said he would 'think about it.'

I discussed the situation with the daughter of the protected person and apologized greatly. She was so gracious that she said it was not a big deal, and that she had plenty of other memorabilia from her father's coaching career.

I was fortunate that there was no claim against the estate. This could have gone very badly for us, but the daughter understood and did not pursue a claim against us. We would have needed to reimburse the estate for the value of the watch and, worse yet, possibly additional funds for the significance of the item to the family heritage.

Be sure you review all items going up for sale in an estate sale before the sale. Pull anything that might be personal to the family. Don't take any chances and don't assume the estate sale company understands what you need as a fiduciary.

Needless to say, we never used that company again.

If you are appointed as trustee of a trust, manage it professionally whether you are a professional or layman. By that, you should do an annual report to the beneficiaries and their counsel. Include a balance sheet of the trust, a profit and loss statement, copies of the bank statements, copies of checks available upon request, and a budget for the trust. Show that you are able to track every cent in and out of the trust and that you are planning how the trust funds will be used in the future. Even if you have to hire a CPA or bookkeeper to prepare the reports, it is well worth the time and expense to report the financial condition of the trust accurately and professionally.

Chapter 4
Conservator

A conservator is a person appointed by a court to manage the financial affairs of a protected, or vulnerable, person. In California and other states, a conservator can be appointed over the finances of a person or of the person, such as the conservator of John Doe. This would be similar to a healthcare representative or a guardian. In Oregon, a conservator is only appointed over the financial affairs of a person, not the person themselves. That would be called a guardianship. For purposes of this book, we will focus on a conservatorship appointment as that being over the financial affairs and _not_ the person.

Need for Appointment

A conservatorship is appointed over a vulnerable person if the person is considered to be 'financially incapable' and is at risk of dissipating or losing assets. Financially incapable means a condition in which a person is unable to manage financial resources of the person effectively for reasons including, but not limited to,

- mental illness
- mental retardation
- physical illness or disability (dementia, stroke, etc)
- chronic use of drugs or controlled substances
- chronic intoxication
- confinement
- detention by a foreign power
- or disappearance.

'Manage financial resources' means those actions necessary to obtain, administer, and dispose of real and personal property, intangible property, business property, benefits and income.

Each state has their own definition of what it means to be financially incapable or unable to manage financial affairs, and the criteria needed to pursue an appointment as conservator. It is important to know what is defined in your jurisdiction before you petition because the petition must speak directly to the statute authorizing the appointment of a conservator and the need for a conservatorship.

To give you an idea of why a conservatorship may be needed, here are a few examples.

Case 1 - An 82 year old man is having difficulty paying his bills on time. He lives alone and has no close family to help. He is in good health, but evidence shows that his utility bills have consistently been late and he is at risk of having his utilities turned off. His house is in poor condition because of deferred maintenance. His roof is leaking and causing severe damage inside a room that he never uses. There was a small fire in the ceiling of the bathroom caused by a fan and never repaired. His property taxes are several years past due and he is at risk of having the house go into foreclosure and a sale forced upon him to pay the taxes. Neighbors have been concerned for his welfare because they see the house deteriorating. They called Adult Protective Services who conducted an investigation and discovered he had not paid many of his bills for many months. Mail was piled up on the table and boxes full of mail were scattered throughout the house.

The man needs a conservator to bring the debts current, to track the man's income, to do maintenance on the house, and to pay for companion service for him to stay in his home as long as possible.

Case 2 – An elderly woman who lives alone recently took in a roommate she met at a soup kitchen. The roommate assisted the woman with her finances for a year, writing checks for her to sign, taking her to the bank, and doing shopping for her. The roommate gained her trust and soon was appointed a power of attorney for her to 'make the job easier' for them both. The investment company at the credit union noticed large withdrawals occurring by the power of attorney and contacted the woman. She said she was aware of the situation because the woman was transferring funds to another institution for better returns. The investment broker contacted Adult

Protective Services who conducted an investigation and discovered more than $400,000 was withdrawn in eighteen months. The power of attorney fled to Texas. A conservatorship may be needed to protect the remaining assets and to pursue charges and a claim against the power of attorney.

<u>Case 3</u> – An elderly couple live in their home on a large farm. They have four adult children who help them occasionally with housekeeping, shopping, and general medical assistance. The couple both have significant dementia and are declining in health.

One of the adult children convince the parents to rewrite their will and leave everything to her. The adult child also gets the parents to make her power of attorney. The adult child soon starts moving personal property out of the house to her house and a storage unit. The other children discover valuable items missing from the house and confront the sibling. She states she is now power of attorney and executor of their will and in charge of her parents' financial affairs, and that she can do anything she wants. The children contact an attorney to determine what options are available. The attorney decides to petition for a conservatorship to investigate the actions, protect the remaining assets, and pursue a claim against the daughter.

The cases show that the underlying reason for a conservatorship appointment is that the persons are vulnerable, someone took advantage of them or they were unable to effectively manage their financial affairs, and, therefore, at risk of loss or dissipation of assets.

Authority of the Conservator

A conservatorship is a much higher level than a power of attorney or trust. A conservatorship removes all financial authority from the protected person (the conservatee) and gives it to the conservator. In essence, the conservator stands in the shoes of the protected person. The conservator takes possession of <u>all</u> assets of the protected person and manages them for the benefit of the protected person. The protected person is unable to open accounts, enter into contracts, obtain loans, or conduct any financial agreement of any kind. Their right to do so has been completely removed from them. The conservator has absolute authority over every aspect of the protected person's finances. Typically, a conservatorship order will revoke any powers of attorney that might be in place.

Upon appointment, the conservator has power to do some tasks without court approval, and some tasks only with court approval. To give you an example, I have detailed the tasks that a conservator is authorized to do with and without court approval in Oregon. The list applies to both professional and laymen conservators.

Tasks a Conservator may do *without* court approval (Oregon)[5]

(1) A conservator may expend or distribute income or principal of the estate without prior court authorization or confirmation for the support, education, care or benefit of the protected person and the dependents of the protected person after the conservator considers recommendations relating to the appropriate standard of support, education, care and benefit for the protected person made by any parent or guardian of the protected person.

(2) A conservator may expend or distribute income or principal of the estate without prior court authorization or confirmation for the support, education, care or benefit of the protected person and the dependents of the protected person if those amounts are reasonably necessary for the support, education, care or benefit of the protected person with due regard to:

    a.   The size of the estate, the probable duration of the conservatorship and the likelihood that the protected person, at some future time, may be fully able to manage the affairs of the protected person and the estate that has been conserved for the protected person;

    b.   The accustomed standard of living of the protected person and members of the household of the protected person; and

    c.   Other funds or sources used for the support of the protected person.

---

[5] **Oregon Revised Statutes (ORS) 125.425 Powers of conservator to pay expenses of protected person and dependents.**

(3) A conservator may expend or distribute income or principal of the estate without prior court authorization or confirmation for the support, education, care or benefit of the dependents of the protected person, other persons who are members of the protected person's household who are unable to support themselves and who are in need of support, and any other persons who were receiving support from the protected person before the appointment of the conservator.

(4) The conservator may reimburse any person, including the protected person, who has expended funds for the purposes specified in this section. The conservator may pay any person in advance for those purposes if the conservator reasonably believes that the services will be performed and where advance payments are customary or reasonably necessary under the circumstances.

To summarize, the conservator can manage the entire financial affairs of the protected person for the benefit of the protected person or members of the protected person's household who are unable to support themselves, are in need of support, and have been supported by the protected person prior to appointment. As conservator, you manage and use the estate to provide for support, education and care. Every decision needs to be weighed against that standard.

To give you an idea of specifically what tasks a conservator can do without court approval, here is a partial list[6];

- Collect, hold and retain assets of the estate including land wherever situated, until, in the judgment of the conservator, disposition of the assets should be made. Assets of the estate may be retained even though those assets include property in which the conservator is personally interested.
- Receive additions to the estate.
- Continue or participate in the operation of any business or other enterprise.

---

[6] **Oregon Revise Statutes (ORS) 125.445 Acts authorized to be performed without prior court approval.**

- Acquire an undivided interest in an estate asset in which the conservator, in any fiduciary capacity, holds an undivided interest.
- Invest and reinvest estate assets and funds in the same manner as a trustee may invest and reinvest.
- Deposit estate funds in a bank including a bank operated by the conservator.
- Acquire or dispose of an estate asset including real property wherever situated for cash or on credit, at public or private sale except the principle residence of the protected person.
- Manage, develop, improve, exchange, partition, change the character of or abandon an estate asset in connection with the exercise of any power vested in the conservator.
- Make ordinary or extraordinary repairs or alterations in buildings or other structures, demolish any improvements, or raze existing or erect new party walls or buildings.
- Subdivide, develop or dedicate land to public use, make or obtain the vacation of plats and adjust boundaries, adjust differences in valuation on exchange or partition by giving or receiving considerations, and dedicate easements to public use without consideration.
- Enter for any purpose into a lease as lessor or lessee with or without option to purchase or renew for a term within or extending beyond the term of the conservatorship.
- Enter into a lease or arrangement for exploration and removal of minerals or other natural resources or enter into a pooling or unitization agreement.
- Grant an option involving disposition of an estate asset or take an option for acquisition of any asset.
- Vote a security, in person or by general or limited proxy.
- Pay calls, assessments and any other sums chargeable or accruing against or on account of securities.
- Sell or exercise stock subscription or conversion rights, or consent, directly or through a committee or other agent, to the reorganization, consolidation, merger, dissolution or liquidation of a corporation or other business enterprise.

- Hold a security in the name of a nominee or in other form without disclosure of the conservatorship so that title to the security may pass by delivery. The conservator is liable for any act of the nominee in connection with the stock so held.
- Insure the assets of the estate against damage or loss, and the conservator against liability with respect to third persons.
- Borrow money to be repaid from estate assets or otherwise and mortgage or pledge property of the protected person as security therefor.
- Advance money for the protection of the estate or the protected person, and for all expenses, losses and liability sustained in the administration of the estate or because of the holding or ownership of any estate assets. The conservator has a lien on the estate as against the protected person for advances so made.
- Pay or contest any claim, settle a claim by or against the estate or the protected person by compromise, arbitration or otherwise, and release, in whole or in part, any claim belonging to the estate to the extent that the claim is uncollectible.
- Pay taxes, assessments, compensation of the conservator and other expenses incurred in the collection, care, administration and protection of the estate.
- Allocate items of income or expense to either income or principal, including creation of reserves out of income for depreciation, obsolescence or amortization, or for depletion in mineral or timber properties.
- Pay any sum distributable to a protected person or a dependent of a protected person by paying the sum to the protected person or the dependent, or by paying the sum either to a guardian, custodian or conservator of the protected person or, if none, to a relative or other person with custody of the protected person.
- Employ persons, including attorneys, auditors, investment advisers or agents, even though they are associated with the conservator, to advise or assist the conservator in the performance of administrative duties, acting upon their recommendation without independent investigation, and instead of acting personally, employing one or more agents to perform any act of administration, whether or not

discretionary, except that payment to the conservator's attorney of record is subject to court approval.

- Prosecute or defend actions, claims or proceedings in any jurisdiction for the protection of estate assets and of the conservator in the performance of duties.
- Prosecute claims of the protected person including those for the personal injury of the protected person.
- Execute and deliver all instruments that will accomplish or facilitate the exercise of the powers vested in the conservator.

Summarized, almost anything financial!

There are some tasks that a conservator may do *only* with court approval.

Tasks a Conservator may do *with* court approval (Oregon)[7]

(1) Convey or release contingent or expectant interests of the protected person in property, including marital property rights and any right of survivorship incident to joint tenancy or tenancy by the entirety.

(2) Create revocable or irrevocable trusts of property of the estate. A trust created by the conservator may extend beyond the period of disability of the protected person or beyond the life of the protected person. A trust created by the conservator must be consistent with the will of the protected person or any other written or oral expression of testamentary intent made by the protected person before the person became incapacitated. The court may not approve a trust that has the effect of terminating the conservatorship unless:

    (a) The trust is created for the purpose of qualifying the protected person for needs-based government benefits or maintaining the eligibility of the protected person for needs-based government benefits;

    (b) The value of the conservatorship estate, including the amount to be transferred to the trust, does not exceed $50,000;

---

[7] **Oregon Revised Statutes (ORS) 125.440 Acts conservator may perform only with court approval.**

    (c) The purpose of establishing the conservatorship was to create the trust; or

    (d) The conservator shows other good cause to the court.

(3) Exercise rights of the protected person to elect options and change beneficiaries under insurance and annuity policies and to surrender the policies for their cash value.

(4) Disclaim any interest the protected person may have by testate or intestate succession, by inter vivos transfer or by transfer on death deed.

(5) Authorize, direct or ratify any annuity contract or contract for life care.

(6) Revoke a transfer on death deed.

(7) Sell the protected person's principle residence.

You can see that the authority of a conservator is significant.

Each state has their own laws regarding conservatorships. A conservator must understand the provisions and limits of their authority and operate within the boundaries set by the law.

Limited Conservatorship

In some instances, a limited conservatorship might be appropriate to protect a vulnerable person. This is when the scope of authority of the conservatorship is limited, not the duration. For example, a person might have a debilitating health condition that would cause them to be financially incompetent for a limited period. Maybe they were incarcerated. They could be prisoners of war and out of the country. There could be a medical condition causing incapacity for a limited duration. An entertainment star could have a significant amount of income in a very short time and have people taking advantage of the situation, causing a dissipation of assets. A person could have a complicated financial situation that requires a conservatorship, such as creating a subdivision from real property owned by the protected person. Or possibly the purpose of the conservatorship is specifically to establish a trust, such as a special needs trust, for a disabled person. In each of these situations, the court would need to review the petition, review the evidence, review the capacity of the protected person, and rule on the appropriateness of a limited conservatorship.

Temporary Conservatorship

Sometimes a temporary conservatorship is appropriate for a certain situation. Often, when a party suspects someone is taking advantage of a vulnerable person, a temporary, or emergency, conservatorship can be appointed. The purpose of the temporary is spelled out in the petition and ruled by the court. The temporary conservator might seek authority to conduct a complete investigation of the allegation of abuse and report back to the court for determination.

A temporary conservatorship could also be for a situation where the protected person is incapacitated for a short period. This could be similar to a limited, but rather than limit the scope of the authority, the duration is limited.

Another example of a temporary conservatorship would be to establish a trust for a disabled person. The temporary conservatorship is for a limited time and scope. Typically these types of conservatorships are created to establish the trust, and then terminated once the trust is funded.

Process for appointment

Each state has their own laws regarding the process of appointment for a conservator. The process can vary between states or even counties within a state. I'll explain the process that we do in Oregon[8].

Petition - First, a petition must be filed with the court. The state laws explain what must be in the petition and how it is to be filed. Generally, a petitioner files a petition explaining that there is evidence that a conservatorship should be created for a person in need because they are financially incapable of managing their assets. The petition is normally filed by a family member or

---

[8] **Oregon Revised Statutes (ORS) 125.055 Petitions in protective proceedings.**

close friend. This would be someone who has 'standing,' or a reason to file because they are involved. A stranger cannot come forward and file a petition for someone they have no involvement with. They would not have standing to do so.

The petition must detail all interested parties, such as family members, involved friends, medical staff if involved, etc. It must detail the evidence that supports that the person is financially incapable. It must list the proposed conservator, the disclosure of the conservator if a professional fiduciary, the nature of the assets needing protection, and a request, or prayer, for the appointment. If a professional fiduciary is the proposed conservator, the petition should list family members or interested parties and that they are not willing or able to serve, and that the professional is appropriate for this appointment.

An attorney should complete and file the petition on behalf of the petitioner.

Notice - Notice of the petition goes to all identified interested parties and the respondent (person for whom the conservatorship is sought) and explains that there is a review period before the court makes the appointment. If no objection is filed by any parties who were noticed, then the court can rule and make the appointment. If an objection is filed, then a hearing is set for all parties to present their position and evidence as to why the conservatorship should or should not be appointed. In Oregon, the notice period is fifteen days.

Court Visitor - In Oregon, a court visitor is appointed to investigate the appropriateness of the appointment whether an objection is filed or not. The visitor interviews all parties involved with the case, reviews the evidence, and prepares a report to the court regarding the petition and appointment with their recommendation. The opinion of the visitor is weighed heavily by the court in making their determination.

Representation - In some jurisdictions, the judge will appoint an attorney for the respondent, even if they have not asked to have one. This shows that the court takes this matter seriously and is insuring that the rights of the individual are not taken away needlessly. This adds more expense to the process, but it protects the respondent from unnecessary removal of their rights to manage their finances.

Order - Once the notice period has run and a hearing made if appropriate, the judge rules on the appointment. The order is created and authorizes the conservator to obtain a bond, or insurance, for the conservatorship.

Bond – The bond is the insurance for the conservatorship against any misdeeds of the conservator. The amount of the bond is determined by adding the annual income of the estate and any assets that the conservator has access to liquidate. We saw earlier that the principle residence of the protected person cannot be sold unless the court issues an order to do so. This is called a restricted asset. The petitioner can list any assets that they want to have restricted to reduce the amount of the bond and the insurance expense to purchase it.

For example, maybe the protected person has four investment accounts, but only needs one investment account to be liquid to provide for the cost of care for the year. The other three accounts can be restricted, thus reducing the bond amount. If additional funds are needed, the conservator can petition the court to unrestrict all or a portion of any of the restricted assets.

Letters of Conservatorship - Once the bond is obtained, which usually takes a couple of days, then the Letters of Conservatorship are issued. These are the authority for the conservator to act.

Case Study – When I first began my career as a professional fiduciary, I thought the court order was the authority to act. When I got my first court order, I went to the bank and demanded access to the protected person's account. They honored my request and withdrew the funds from the account payable to the conservatorship. This proved to me, erroneously, that the court order was the authority.

On my next appointment, I took the court order to another bank and they refused my request. Confused, I contacted my attorney and asked him to call the bank. He corrected me and explained I had no authority until I received the letters of conservatorship. I went back to the first bank and explained that they had made a mistake by issuing checks to the conservatorship based on the court order. They appreciated my honesty and we have since developed a good relationship working together on the many cases that followed.

The letters of conservatorship are the authority for the conservator to act. Don't do anything until you receive the letters!

First acts of the Conservator

When the conservator is appointed, the very first acts that they should do _on the very first day_ are to protect the assets of the protected person.

Insurance - Verify that all assets are insured. If there is any question, get insurance. If the conservator discovers that insurance already existed, the insurance obtained should be immediately cancelled and a refund sought. Do not accept an appointment as conservator and forget to insure the house of the protected person. If it is uninsured, and a fire happens to breakout, you, as conservator, could be liable for the negligence to obtain insurance. The parties would have a great reason to file a claim against your bond for negligence that resulted in a loss to the estate.

To repeat – insure all assets immediately!

Bank accounts – Send notice to all financial institutions that you are aware of regarding your appointment with copies of the letters of conservatorship and the order. Put them on notice that a conservatorship was created and to freeze all accounts until further notice. Request history of the accounts for the past 30 days. You will be able to review the accounts and determine if any theft might have occurred or if any automated deposits or withdrawals are taking place that need to be changed to the conservatorship account. You will also need the statement copy for your beginning inventory that is filed with the court.

Real Property – If the protected person lives in a facility and has real property that is vacant, then change all of the locks on any real property and install an alarm. Often, the real property has personal property inside. Make sure you have taken appropriate actions to protect the property the best you can, even if you have to hire security to watch it until you can fully inventory and protect it. Install an alarm if you have to.

If the protected person lives in their house, then determine the best solution to protecting the assets the best you can. You might not need to change the locks or install an alarm, but you would need to inventory the personal property as quickly as possible. We find that a quick photoshoot inside the house will provide a detailed record of the majority of the personal property in the house. Take a thousand photos if you have to. Use a good camera so you can blow the photos up and view the details of the assets. Remove any jewelry, precious metals, or documents as quickly as you can and store them in a secure environment, such as a safe or safe deposit box.

Address change – A change of address should be filed with the post office on the first day of appointment. This will enlighten the conservator to any other hidden accounts, income, expenses, and past due bills of the protected person.

Restrict Credit – The conservator should send notification to the local credit bureaus immediately after appointment. The notice should indicate who the conservator is, the name and social security number of the protected person, and the request to restrict or block all credit for the protected person. This will effectively restrict the protected person from obtaining credit and subsequently obtaining any loans or credit cards. The conservator should also request a credit report to see what activity has occurred, what accounts and balances are outstanding, and where unknown assets may be held.

You can see that the first day or two of your appointment is going to be busy and long. Don't take any shortcuts!

Follow up acts of the Conservator

Once the real property, insurance and bank accounts have been controlled, follow up with securing the remaining assets and transferring them into the conservatorship.

Bank accounts/Investments – Change the name on the accounts if possible. Often, financial institutions will not allow you to change names on accounts. Instead, you will need to open new accounts. If you need to open new accounts and transfer the funds, make sure you inquire about beneficiaries on the accounts and structure the new accounts *exactly* as the prior accounts were structured. If at all possible, try to not close or transfer existing accounts with beneficiaries named on them. Just restrict them at the institution level.

Inventory Personal Property – Prepare a detailed photo or video inventory of the personal property as quickly as possible. Take detailed pictures of everything in the house. Open drawers, open boxes, empty items onto a bed for better photos. Be detailed in your recording of the personal property in the house. Sometimes parties (family members) can argue over what you think is the most insignificant item. But to them, it is a treasure. This is the second pass of photos after your appointment. Make sure you are complete and detailed with creating the inventory of the personal property.

Asset search – The photo inventory is a good time to conduct a thorough asset search. A conservator must search through all of the personal property to try and discover any hidden assets. This is a time consuming process that a conservator must pay attention to and conduct personally. Never conduct a search alone. Always work in pairs. If you need to use the services of a contractor, pair them with a fiduciary. Never allow one person to be alone in any area of the house that has not been searched and recorded. If possible, never use a family member, regardless of how good their intentions may be.

Case Study 1 - I was appointed as conservator for a family that had a heritage farm (100 years old) and a lot of valuable, personal items in the house. Many of the more expensive and memorable items were in a safe, such as guns, jewelry, and heirlooms. The son of the protected persons was the guardian for them. I assumed he would be trustworthy since he had a responsibility to account for his actions to the court as did I. I asked him to help me inventory the safe. I explained it would cost the estate less, and that he could explain the history of some of the items. I thought it would be a good process for us to work together. He sat on the bed as I took pictures of each item and handed it to him to comment on and set aside. When we finished, we put everything back in the safe and locked it up.

No one had a combination to the safe but my staff, and no one went to the house except me or my senior case manager.

When the protected persons passed away, about two years later, the son became the personal representative and was entitled to control all of the remaining assets of the conservatorship. I transferred the bank accounts and titles to him. Then, we went to the house and I opened the safe. We compared every item in the safe to the pictures. To my surprise, a gold watch was missing. It happened to be the same gold watch that he made several comments on when we inventoried the safe together. The value of the watch was only $150. It was an insignificant asset from my perspective. I believe he pocketed the watch when I temporarily turned my back to get something out of the safe. I couldn't prove it, but I knew it.

Besides being outraged that he set me up to accuse me of theft, I was extremely hurt. My confidence in myself and trust in people was attacked.

I settled by paying the estate $750 for the watch, which is what he said it was worth.

Lesson learned – don't trust _anyone_ to conduct an inventory with you. Even then, keep everyone and every asset in sight at all times! You are ultimately on the hook if something comes up missing!

Be sure to search everywhere!

- Open food items in the freezer and cupboard
- Look through the newspapers and trash
- Open seat cushions
- Look under and behind furniture for taped items
- Thumb through books for currency and notes
- Look through clothes pockets for currency
- Use metal detectors if you suspect precious metals are hidden underground, in the walls, under carpet, etc.
- Open picture frames

Case Study 2 - To give you an idea of what could happen during an asset search, here is another case that will shock you. I was conservator for a man who lived on some acreage. There were rumors that he had hidden some gold on the grounds. When we began searching assets, we found $1.4 million in gold, silver and cash. These assets were discovered in chicken coops, trash piles, candy jars, hidden compartments, buried; anywhere you could imagine! It took four of us a full week to search the majority of the grounds.

We finally retained the services of a metal detection group to finish the search under close supervision. Our agreement was that they could keep anything under $1,000 in value, and 10% of anything above. They did not find much, but we were assured we looked everywhere we could for assets.

All of this when the protected person virtually lived in, and raised his family, in poverty!

Case Study 3 – We conducted an asset search of an elderly woman who lived in a small house of meager means. In the garage, I searched through the cans and jars of bolts, screws, and miscellaneous hardware. In one can, there was a pile of bolts and nuts with some newspaper at the bottom. I emptied the can and opened the paper. There were several diamond rings and a diamond necklace in the bottom of the can. The appraised value of the jewelry was more than $5,000.

You have no idea what is hidden. Search thoroughly. Search under dual custody. Document everything.

Taxes – The conservator should contact the IRS and State tax agency to obtain the latest tax information from them. This will reveal if the protected person is current with their taxes or not. The information you receive might be complete copies of their tax returns. If the taxes have not been filed in a timely manner, then transcripts of tax activity from financial institutions can be obtained. This will reveal where interest is coming from or being paid to on behalf of the protected person. It is an effective 'back door' to locating unknown or hidden accounts.

Escheated Assets – Occasionally, a person will overlook small balances in obscure accounts. If the protected person has developed severe dementia, the balances could be significantly large. Each state has a website to conduct searches for escheated[9], or forgotten, money. If an account at a financial institution is left for more than a year, those funds become dormant and eventually are escheated, or turned over, to the state. The state will maintain a record of escheated funds that can be sought by the conservator. The state website will give instructions on how to obtain those funds.

Financial Institution Inquiry Letters – On occasion, you might decide to send inquiry letters to local financial institutions. Sometimes, a person might open a safe deposit box and prepay it for years, allowing it to just sit there. Be sure to send copies of your letters of conservatorship and the ward's information so they can conduct a search.

Digital Assets – In today's digital world, some people may have assets that are held online or digitally. Here is a partial list:

- Photographs/Stock photography
- Online Auctions – EBay, Amazon, Wish
- PayPal
- Bitcoin
- Website – sales, crafts, products, store

It is important to search the computers of the protected person to determine if digital assets are held somewhere. It can be most difficult trying to obtain the assets without passwords or online access. Each vendor has their own process and requirements.

Other assets – Occasionally, you might come across an estate where other assets may be held that you are not familiar with. Here is a partial list of what you could discover;

---

[9] **Escheated** – A process where a financial institution turns forgotten money or assets over to the state for holding and processing.

- Original artwork for movies/cartoons
- Recorded albums
- Original films
- Patents
- Copyrighted material – books, songs, prints
- Original Art
- Real property
- Timeshare

Any of these types of assets are extremely difficult to manage, protect and asses for insurance purposes or liquidation. Do not hesitate to contact a professional to assist you with securing and protecting these assets.

Case Study 1 – I was appointed as conservator for an elderly lady who had no children or relatives. She lived in a small apartment in a facility. We were appointed through an investigation by Adult Protective Services. We conducted a general asset search with her help. Since she was the only person in the apartment, and had no family, we did not search as thoroughly as we probably should have. Regardless, we believed we had enough information to protect the assets for her estate.

About a year later, she passed away. We were going through her items in great detail and discovered in a booklet some artwork. They were the original foils for Dumbo, a Walt Disney movie. We discovered the lady was an artist for Walt Disney when she first began her career!

We had no idea of the value of the foils, and did not research them very much. I contacted the sole beneficiary of her estate, a charitable organization, and asked if they wanted us to pursue research. They said no and asked if we could just deliver the foils. We did, and they were elated!

You never know what you will find!

Case Study 2 – I was appointed conservator for a couple who had a daughter who was power of attorney for her parents. She asked us to be conservator and take over the estate because she was in another state, and there were no other siblings to help. We conducted an inventory and found that the parents had a fractional interest of ownership in a timeshare condominium. They owned 1/64th of a very large condominium complex used as a timeshare. The daughter said she completed some paperwork to get rid of the condominium interest and stop the periodic dues.

I contacted the timeshare liquidation company the daughter hired to sell the condominium interest and notified them that I was appointed conservator for the couple and that her power of attorney had been revoked. I asked for supporting paperwork to show the condominium interest was no longer in the protected persons' names. They sent the paperwork to me which I reviewed. What I discovered was that the company sold the condominium immediately after my appointment and forged the signatures of the protected persons at a time they were under conservatorship. Not only that, they sold the fractional interest for $10.00 (yes, ten dollars) to two people who happened to be owners of the company who was hired to liquidate the interest of the protected persons! I easily verified this by searching through the online business registrations in that state and gathered the information of who the president, secretary, and owners of the company were.

Talk about a conflict of interest!

I contacted the company and demanded they reverse the transaction and put the condominium back into the names of the protected persons. They did, and I was able to sell the fractional interest in the condominium for $30,000. I also got the $250 the daughter paid the liquidation company to sell the interest.

I turned all of my information over to the state attorney general's office in the state the company was operating in after I was paid.

Don't take anything for granted. Understand the nature of the assets, the history, and be thorough with your investigation.

Inventory – The conservator is required to file an inventory with the court within 60 days of appointment. This could vary between states. The inventory should list all of the assets under conservatorship from the date of appointment.

Annual Accounting – The conservator is required to provide an annual accounting of the conservatorship. This report will detail all of the income received, expenses paid, bank statements, investment statements, check copies, copies of deed, property values, vehicles, and any assets received or disposed of over the past year. Each state has their rules about the accounting, but generally speaking, it is a complete financial report of the conservatorship. For a professional fiduciary, it should look very similar to a business financial report with a balance sheet, profit and loss report, with supporting detail of every entry.

It must balance to the penny and must balance to the latest bank statement(s).

Consideration for a fiduciary –We often provide a 'Report of the Conservator' to accompany the accounting on complicated cases. The report should explain any unusual events during the accounting period. It helps to highlight significant issues that may have arisen and relate that to the conservator's billing, such as the investigation of the fractional interest in the condominium that resulted in an additional $30,000 of discovered assets.

I believe it is better to provide too much information to the court rather than too little. If the court doesn't need or want it, they will tell you. Your attorney will aid you with gathering the information and preparing it for the court.

Managing the Estate Plan

The conservator must manage the conservatorship based on the estate plan of the protected person. The estate plan is understood by gathering as much information as you can about the nature of the assets, the structure of the bank and investment accounts, and any memorialized wishes of the protected person, such as a will or trust.

If the protected person has a bank account, and has designated a beneficiary on the account, such as a 'payable on death' (POD) account, then the conservator must consider that designation when they are spending the assets of the estate. The conservator should use undesignated accounts first for spending, and designated accounts last after the estate plan is fully understood. This way, they will not spend any one beneficiary's potential inheritance first, but insure all beneficiary's interests are spent equally.

For example, let's assume a conservatorship is appointed, the protected person has three children and no other beneficiaries, and there is no will. When the person dies, state law directs that each child would receive one-third of the remaining estate. If there is an account that is designated POD to one of three children, then that account should be used *last*. The undesignated accounts should be used first since all three would have their shares each reduced evenly. If we spent from the designated account first, that child would lose a larger share of the future inheritance than the other two children. That could set you up for a claim against you for breach of fiduciary duty by depriving them of their rightful inheritance, especially if *your* account was the one preserved!

The conservator must gather all of the beneficiary information about every account and asset. Is the account joint? Is it designated POD or have a beneficiary named on it? Is there a will that devises specific assets to a beneficiary? If any of these situations exist, those assets must be used *last*.

Case Study - I once had a case that was quite complicated. The will designated 18 beneficiaries of various assets; cars, accounts, stuffed animals, the farm etc. I had some undesignated funds available to pay bills, but I was running low on cash and needed to come up with a plan to spend down every beneficiary evenly.

I had appraisals done by professionals on every designated asset. The car, farm, and other assets were simple. Even the personal property was pretty easy. The difficult asset to appraise were the 50+ stuffed animals in the house. Many of the animals, such as deer, mountain lions, and a bear, were full, life size mounts! The protected person was an avid hunter. I contacted an insurance company who was able to appraise the stuffed animals based on the cost a person would have to pay for a guided hunt. Remarkably, the value of the stuffed animals exceeded $100,000. We were able to insure the animals and include them in the inventory and estate spend down plan. We later petitioned the court to distribute them to the beneficiary (a museum). The other beneficiaries did not object, the court approved the distribution, and the *animals were moved to the museum and removed from the inventory. We also petitioned to give the car to the beneficiary, thus eliminating all non-liquid assets, except the farm.*

We petitioned the court to liquidate all of the remaining accounts and explained how we planned to maintain the integrity of the protected person's estate plan by depositing all of the assets into a single account with percentages of beneficiaries designated on the account. This gave every beneficiary an opportunity to object to our plan. No one objected. The remaining accounts were liquidated and deposited into a single account. The percentage of each beneficiary's interest in the one account was calculated. Each beneficiary was added to the account with their beneficial interest. So, there were sixteen beneficiaries on one account each with a percentage of interest payable on death. Then, as I spent from the account, each person lost the same relative value of their inheritance.

The farm, however, was a different issue. We had the farm appraised and obtained a large line of credit. As I needed cash for management of the conservatorship and payment for the protected person's 24-hour in-home care, I drew the same relative percentage of the value of the farm on the line of credit that I spent on the account. For example, if I spent 10% of the bank account balance, I drew 10% <u>of the value of the farm</u> on the line of credit. The beneficiary of the farm was pretty upset because I was running up a large loan that he would have to assume upon the death of the protected person. It was fair because he stood to receive the largest asset.

When the protected person passed away, the personal representative settled the estate, and we had no claims filed against us as conservator. My plan worked!

It is imperative that you, as conservator, understand the structure and estate plan of the protected person and manage the conservatorship accordingly to avoid future claims or litigation against you.

Use of Conservatorship Funds

The assets of the conservatorship should only be used for the benefit of the protected person. It is important for the conservator to learn who the protected person is, their history, their interests, likes, dislike and habits. The conservator may need to depend on a guardian or other family members to educate them about the protected person and their interests. The conservator should use the protected person's funds only for the protected person to support, educate, maintain, and enhance their quality of life.

Case Study – We were appointed conservator for an elderly Japanese woman. Her husband passed away and they had no close relatives or friends. All of her relatives lived in Japan.

The woman spoke broken English. She lived in a facility and seemed to be doing OK, but was not 'thriving.' We hired a Japanese translator as a companion. She met with our ward every week and took her out for an authentic Japanese meal. Our client improved and did much better.

Then, I got an idea.

I petitioned the court to allow us to use the protected person's funds to fly some relatives from Japan to Oregon to visit with our client. The court approved my petition and we established a regular trip twice a year for relatives to fly from Japan to Oregon and meet with our client. After the first visit, our client's health improved remarkably.

The purpose of managing the finances of the conservatorship is for the benefit of the protected person.

The conservatorship may also be used for dependents if the protected person had a history of supporting that dependent. This will be explained in the law of your jurisdiction of appointment. Always check with your attorney if you are unsure.

The protected person may also provide input for the conservator to consider. The purpose of the conservatorship is to protect the person from dissipating their assets; not to preserve the assets for future beneficiaries.

Prudent Investor/Conserve Assets

A conservator should be cautious about how they manage the estate and the investments of the protected person. It would be inappropriate for a conservator to seek risky investments. The conservator should employ the expertise of investment managers to help create a financial plan to sustain the level of care and quality of life the protected person should enjoy without adding excessive risk to the investment portfolio.

Case Study 1– I was appointed successor conservator behind a conservator who was a certified public accountant. He was also a friend of the protected person. After my appointment, I secured, or marshalled, the assets of the estate. There was a single investment account with a hundred thousand dollars in it. I noticed the majority of the investments were in a few, high risk equities, or stocks. I questioned the investments and contacted the investment manager. He began rattling off how great the investments were because 'they were going to pay big really soon.'

I was uncomfortable with his investment plan, so I transferred the assets to a new broker along with an investment policy I created for the estate. I detailed anticipated cashflow needs to help pay for the protected person's care.

Later, I researched the historical activity of the prior investment broker. I obtained two years of statements and discovered the portfolio lost over 50% of its value during that time. I contacted an investment attorney who confirmed the investments were very high risk and, from a conservator's perspective, highly inappropriate to have in the portfolio. The protected person was only fifty years old and needed the investments to supplement her care payments.

I filed a claim against the prior conservator and investment broker. They settled for a cash payment of over $100,000 to replenish the conservatorship.

Be careful how your broker invests the funds of the conservatorship. If you do not know what the investments are or the risks they pose, don't get them.

Case Study 2– On another case, I was appointed conservator and, again, I secured the assets of the estate and began researching some historical activity. The estate was that of a farmer who understood very little about investments. His wealth came from a settlement where his son was accidentally electrocuted at work. The funds were deposited with a reputable firm with a large percentage in equities, or stocks.

As I researched some of the historical fees and costs, I discovered the broker was 'churning' the account; he was buying and selling investments almost daily. Over a year, the broker earned $12,000 of transaction fees on a $50,000 portfolio. I contacted the company and filed a complaint. The broker was adamant that he did nothing wrong because he contacted the farmer, now a protected person with advanced dementia, regarding every transaction. There was nothing I could really do except file a complaint with the SEC. Nothing came out of it, except I will never use that company again.

Case Study 3– I was appointed as trustee for an elderly man who was terminally ill. He had a broker who had been managing his financial investment for several years. When I took over the investments, I questioned many of them. The broker was purchasing high commission annuities, real estate investment trusts, and collateralized mortgages. The investments were scattered with numerous companies. Letters from the broker to the man were not on letterhead, did not indicate the broker was licensed, and did not contain a combined investment recap with estimated values or estimated cash flows. In summary, it looked like a kid in high school typed out a letter and mailed it.

I was shocked. I researched the broker and discovered he had worked at four different organizations in the past six years. He also had a complaint for misrepresentation and a settlement for $70,000. I tried to meet with the broker at his office that was indicated on his SEC file. The office was empty and there were no signs. I was unable to ever meet with the broker, though I tried several times. I discovered he was a broker for many of the elderly persons in this particular manufactured home community.

The beneficiary of the trust passed away and I settled the estate. I could not see any theft by the broker. What I saw was a broker who was buying and selling risky, high expense investments to elderly people in a very unprofessional manner. He was misrepresenting who he was and his employment.

I filed a complaint with the Security Exchange Commission. Nothing came of it, other than a complaint is on his record. He never responded, though the company he worked for did. They sent me a letter stating the broker left their employment and that they could not comment on his past activities other than those that relate to policy.

You, as a fiduciary, need to use caution with every broker you encounter. Some are just not ethical. Do your homework. Understand investments. Research some historical activity after appointment. Manage the investments with a close eye on what the broker is doing. Be cautious and prudent with your investments. Don't try and 'shoot the moon' and reach for huge gains. Instead, be conservative, protect the assets, and obtain a reasonable return on the portfolio. Your protected person depends on it.

Termination of the conservatorship

A conservatorship can be terminated for the following reasons;

- Death of the protected person
- The protected person becomes financially capable
- The conservatorship runs out of funds (typically less than $10,000)

Emergency or Temporary Conservatorships

Occasionally, there is a need for a temporary or emergency conservatorship. They are both the same, but often named differently in different jurisdictions. For purposes of this writing, we will refer to just the temporary conservatorship.

A temporary conservatorship is sought for a short, limited period because of an event or situation that needs immediate attention. This typically involves a vulnerable person, such as an elderly person with dementia, a developmentally disabled person, someone with brain injury or mental illness, etc. Some of the possible reasons for a temporary conservatorship are:

- A person is being taken advantage of through theft or misuse of funds.
- A person is being evicted from a facility for non-payment.
- An event occurs that leaves the person's fiduciary unable to perform, such as an arrest or death.
- A person is unable to perform their financial duties due to illness (coma, injury, etc).

In these and other situations, the need is immediate and the situation dire. Often, these types of cases arise through Adult Protective Services, a facility, law enforcement or hospitals. The process is the same as a conventional conservatorship. The court requires evidence that a conservatorship is immediately needed. Once presented, the court can approve the conservatorship without the normal fifteen day notice and appoint a conservator for a limited time, normally 30 days.

During that period, the temporary conservator has the full authority of a conventional conservator, but only for the limited time. The court will send a court visitor after the appointment to gather more information for the court. At the end of thirty days, either the conservatorship is terminated or a conventional conservatorship is created. Often, when a temporary conservatorship petition is filed, it includes language to create a conventional conservatorship at the expiration of the temporary. This allows the temporary conservator to take control of the estate, conduct an investigation, resolve the immediate crisis, and continue as a regular conservatorship appointment with proper notice to the parties involved. An objection for the conventional conservatorship could be filed and a hearing held while the temporary conservatorship is active.

Often, a temporary conservatorship can be, and is, extended for an additional thirty days to manage the affairs of the protected person and prepare for the conventional appointment.

The responsibilities and acts of the temporary conservator are the same as a conventional conservator. The only difference is that the temporary conservator addresses the immediate crisis and resolves it.

Case Study – A woman was in a facility and failed to pay her $7,000 per month bill. She had her son as power of attorney, but the bill started to get behind. An eviction notice was sent to her son who disregarded it and failed to bring the balance current. The facility contacted Adult Protective Services (APS) because the woman was facing eviction, and no facility wants to evict an elderly, disabled person.

APS also contacted the police because they suspected the son was committing financial elder abuse as well by using the woman's funds. The police began an investigation while we petitioned for appointment to see what was going on. The court approved the appointment of the temporary to head off the eviction, and called a hearing on the conventional appointment because the son objected.

Our investigation revealed the son had spent more than $100,000 of the woman's funds while neglecting to pay her facility bill. He was the only child, so his reasoning was that he was going to inherit her estate anyway, and her health was declining.

The court appointed us as permanent conservator and we put a case together for the police to seek prosecution of the son for financial elder abuse. The son was convicted and sentenced to five years in prison. The truly sad part of this case was that the mother passed away six months after the son was incarcerated and the prison would not allow him to go to his mother's funeral.

If you are appointed as a temporary conservator, be sure to research the recent historical activity for any potential theft. You were appointed for a reason. Be thorough in your research.

Considerations for a fiduciary

A fiduciary is under close scrutiny by the court and interested parties when they become a conservator for a protected person.

- Be sure to protect all of the assets you can immediately upon appointment.
- Inventory all of the assets in _dual custody_.
- Do not seek risky investments. Create a budget and spending plan and have a competent investment broker discuss the options with you. Evaluate the plan semi-annually and adjust accordingly.
- Act on behalf of the protected person for every action.
- Document all of your activity and record every transaction in detail.
- Retain professionals to help you manage the case. If you don't think you can manage it, don't take the appointment.
- When it comes to conservatorships and vulnerable persons, I have discovered one thing_; it's always about the Benjamins_ ($100 bills). You will may be involved in a case where people are fighting over money. Don't be surprised. Remain neutral.

Chapter 5
Personal Representative/Executor

Another area that professional fiduciaries get appointed to regularly is that of the personal representative or executor of an estate.

When a person passes away, their estate is subject to distribution to the heirs of the estate, whether they have an estate plan or not. If the person has a trust, as previously explained, the distribution plan of the trust assets at the time of death of the beneficiary is well defined and can be executed without court intervention. That is why most trusts are created; to avoid the probate of an estate.

Probate

Probate is a legal process whereby a court oversees the distribution of assets left by a deceased person. Assets are anything a person owns with value, such as real and personal property and cash. An estate is probated, or closed through a court process, when there is no estate plan, called intestate, or if the estate plan is a will. In Oregon, an estate can be closed different ways depending on the value of the assets of the estate, also known as the size of the estate. Each state has their own rules. Be sure to understand the rules of your state.

Probate is not always necessary. If the deceased person owned bank accounts or property with another person, the surviving co-owner will then own that property automatically when the person passes away if the ownership of the account is structured to do so, like 'joint with right of survivorship, or 'payable on death.' The co-owner needs to provide a copy of the death certificate to the financial institution and the account is transferred into the name of the co-owner. If a person dies leaving very few assets, such as personal belongings or household goods, these items can be distributed among the rightful beneficiaries without the supervision of the court.

Sometimes probate is needed to:

- Clear title to land, stocks and bonds, or large bank or savings and loan accounts that were held in the name of the deceased person only, and put the title to these assets in the names of the rightful beneficiaries.
- Collect debts owed to the deceased person.
- Settle a dispute between people who claim they are entitled to assets of the deceased person.
- Resolve any disputes about the validity of the deceased person's will.

The Process

If the deceased person had a will, the will is "proved" and delivered to the court. The deceased person's will can be proved by an affidavit made under oath by the witnesses to the will. If such an affidavit is unavailable, the personal presence of the witnesses may be required in court to testify that at the time the will was signed, the deceased person was of sound mind and knew what he or she was doing.

A personal representative, or executor, is selected to handle the deceased person's affairs. A will generally names a personal representative who, if willing to serve and otherwise qualified, will be approved by the court. If a person dies without a will, called intestate, the court will select the personal representative who is usually the spouse, an adult child or other close relative of the deceased person. If none of those people are available or willing to be the personal representative, the court may choose a bank, trust company, lawyer, or professional fiduciary.

A notice to creditors is published in a local newspaper. This public notice tells the creditors that they have four months to bring any claim against the estate for debts that the deceased person owes them. The personal representative also gives written notice to all known and possible creditors.

The heirs and people named in the will are notified of the probate proceeding. If there is no will, the heirs according to the laws of the state are notified, such as children, siblings, etc.

The personal representative works to identify and value the deceased person's assets and prepare an inventory to the court. Depending upon the type of assets and the kind of records left by the deceased person, this step can be quite straightforward — or difficult and time consuming.

Case Study – I was appointed as conservator for an elderly woman. It was an emergency conservatorship that resulted in a permanent appointment. The woman had no children and no siblings. No one was involved with her care even though she was living alone in her house. She was 98 years old.

When she passed away, we petitioned to be the claiming successor of her small estate (see the chapter on personal representative/executor). There was a few thousand dollars in her estate that needed to be distributed to her legal beneficiaries. Since she had no will or trust, we had to determine who her beneficiaries were. What we discovered was a personal representative's nightmare.

The woman had no children or siblings (immediate family members). The law states you go fist to immediate family members and, if there are none, then you go up to the lineage of the parents and their siblings, and then back down through all of their descendants. The woman's mother had ten siblings. Her father had eleven siblings. They were born more than 120 years ago. That means that all of the family members born to all twenty-one siblings, and their descendants over the last 120 years, were entitled to a share of the estate.

We stopped searching after we passed a hundred people.

There was no feasible way that we would be able to conduct a thorough enough search of her descendants. We turned the case, and assets, over to the state to process the estate.

The personal representative ensures that creditors are paid. Creditors must be repaid from the estate before the remaining estate assets can be distributed to the rightful beneficiaries.

The personal representative prepares state and/or federal tax returns and any inheritance, gift and estate tax returns and pays any taxes due.

The personal representative prepares and submits an account to the people named in the will; the heirs of the deceased person and the court. The account shows all money paid out from the estate and all money collected by the estate. It also contains a narrative explaining the important actions taken in connection with the probate of the estate.

After court approval of the account and payment of all unpaid probate expenses, the deceased person's assets are distributed to the people and entities (such as charities or trusts) named in the will or, if the person died without a will, to the heirs of the deceased person per the rules of law.

Small Estate

Oregon allows an abbreviated procedure for handling small estates that would otherwise require a full probate. If an estate fits in this category, the cost and time for distributing the estate assets may be greatly reduced. The procedure involves filing a document called an "affidavit of claiming successor." This abbreviated procedure can be used if the estate's personal property is valued at no more than $75,000 and real property is valued at no more than $200,000, for a total aggregate estate value of no more than $275,000. (These rates are as of April 2016, but can be changed by the state legislature.) Real property includes land and buildings or structures placed on land, such as houses, commercial buildings and agricultural buildings. Personal property includes all other property, such as cars, boats, clothing, stocks, bonds and personal items.

Personal Property

One of the most difficult assets to distribute in an estate plan, be it a will or trust, is personal property. Though I am repeating myself, I think it is best to reiterate a way to divide the personal property of an estate where the property has not been specifically devised[10] to a beneficiary.

---

[10] **Devised** – When an asset of an estate is specifically left, or given, to a person through a will or trust.

What we do in most cases is hire an estate sale company to sell the personal property of the estate. The estate sale company will come in after we have inventoried and searched the assets and prepared the personal property for an estate sale. The estate sale companies we use will normally charge 30-40% to conduct the sale. They will go through every item, price it, remove all pictures and personal items (anything with a name on it, documents, trophies, etc), and prepare for a sale. Then, we offer the family members to come to the sale for a preview. If they are arguing, then let one person at a time preview the items. They are allowed to select anything they want. The estate sale company will tag it (or list it) and run a total. If two persons want the same thing, we put their names in a bowl and draw for a winner. The total of all of their selected items becomes a part of their distributive share. We have done this on many, many cases successfully. The key here is to detail the process to the beneficiaries, get them to agree, and control the process. This also works well for conservatorships and trusts.

Trusts

Sometimes a person's estate plan is a will that creates a trust for a beneficiary. For example, a person might have a disabled child and leave their estate to a special needs trust for the child. The personal representative must create the trust and fund it with the proceeds of the estate. The trustee would then take control of the assets and manage them under the trust.

Remains

This is the one area of fiduciary management that can become very emotional for the parties involved; the disposition of remains of the deceased person. Hopefully, the estate you are appointed over has a clear request or direction from the person as to what they want done with their remains. If that is the case, just follow their instructions and document well. It helps greatly to communicate that to the beneficiaries as soon as you possibly can.

If there are no directions, and the remains have not been fully decided or acted upon, then query the family to see what they believe the person would have wanted. If you are able to reach a consensus, document the agreement and have each person sign a release and waiver (your attorney can draft one). Then, you are clear to act upon the remains.

If the parties are not in agreement, then it becomes a little sticky. The funeral homes operate under statute that direct them how to proceed. Each state may have their own set of rules for the funeral home to operate under, so be sure to check with them. If the parties and the funeral home are unable to resolve the issue, then you will need to petition the court for instructions.

A petition for instructions is simply gathering the facts, presenting them to the court in the form of a petition stating that the issue is disposition of the remains of the protected person and requesting the court to provide instructions on what to do. The court will call a hearing where all of the parties involved will attend and provide testimony. In the end, the court will rule. This is an excellent way to avoid liability or future litigation because each party has been provided the opportunity to present their case with the court ruling making the decisions.

Chapter 6
Guardian

A guardian is a person who looks after and is legally responsible for someone who is unable to manage their own affairs, especially an incompetent or disabled person or a child whose parents have died. In the realm of a fiduciary, a guardian is someone who manages the person. It is much like a parent is the guardian of a child. The parent makes all of the decisions for the child relating to food, shelter, medical services, education, etc.

A guardian may be appointed for an adult person only as is necessary to promote and protect the well-being of the protected person. A guardianship for an adult person must be designed to encourage the development of maximum self-reliance and independence of the protected person and may be ordered only to the extent necessitated by the person's actual mental and physical limitations.

Guardianships are not simple by any means. The guardian must consider the welfare of the protected person and provide a least restrictive environment that promotes self-determination while insuring safety. This is a difficult balancing act for anyone. If a person suffers from advanced dementia, keeping them safe in a least restrictive environment is a challenge. If they are living at home, when is the right time to move them to a safer, more restrictive environment? Is it after they catch the house on fire, wander down the street in their nightgown during a snowstorm, or before? If before, how much more? You can see that these are not simple issues to address.

Each decision must be weighed against the banner of self-determination and least restrictive alternatives while considering safety. More on this later.

Process for appointment

Each state has their own laws regarding the process of appointment for a guardian. The process can vary even between counties. It is almost identical to that of a conservatorship. Below is the process that we do in Oregon for professional or laymen fiduciaries.

Petition

First, a petition must be filed with the court. The state laws explains what must be in the petition and how it is to be filed. Generally, a petitioner files a petition explaining that there is evidence that a guardianship should be created for a person because they are incapacitated, unable to make medical decisions, and are at risk of injury or death to themselves or others. The petition is normally filed by a family member or close friend. This would be someone who has 'standing,' or a reason to file because they are involved. A stranger cannot come forward and file a petition for someone they have no involvement with. They would not have standing to do so.

The petition must detail all interested parties, such as family members, involved friends, medical staff if involved, etc. It must detail the evidence that supports that the person is incapacitated and include an original letter from a doctor or medical practitioner clearly stating that the person requires a guardian. The petition must list the proposed guardian, the disclosure of the guardian if a professional fiduciary, the nature of impairment or medical need, and a request, or prayer, for the appointment. If a professional fiduciary is the proposed guardian, the petition should list family members or interested parties in the case that are not willing or able to serve, and that the professional fiduciary is appropriate for this appointment. If the person has limited assets and requires the guardian to manage the assets, this should be included in the petition.

It is important to fully disclose all of the relationships and evidence to avoid a conflict of interest, which is explained later in this book. An attorney should complete and file the petition on behalf of the petitioner.

Notice

Notice of the petition goes to all identified interested parties and the respondent (person for whom the guardianship is sought) and explains that there is a review period before the court makes the appointment. If no objection is filed by any parties who were noticed, then the court can rule and make the appointment. If an objection is filed, then a hearing is set for all parties to present their position and evidence as to why the guardianship should or should not be appointed. In Oregon, the notice period is fifteen calendar days.

Court Visitor

In Oregon, a court visitor is appointed to investigate the appropriateness of the appointment whether an objection is filed or not. The visitor interviews all parties involved with the case, reviews the evidence, and prepares a report to the court regarding the petition and appointment with their recommendation. The opinion of the visitor is weighed heavily by the court in making their determination.

Representation

In some jurisdictions, the judge will appoint an attorney for the respondent, even if they have not asked for one. This shows that the court takes this matter seriously and is insuring that the rights of the individual are not taken away needlessly. This adds more expense to the process, but it protects the respondent from unnecessary removal of their rights to manage their healthcare and placement.

Order/Letters of Guardianship

Once the notice period has run and a hearing conducted if appropriate, the judge rules on the appointment. The order is created and authorizes the guardian to act accordingly. A bond is seldom needed in a guardianship unless the guardian is authorized to manage limited funds of the protected person. If a bond is required, it must be obtained before the Letters of Guardianship are issued. These are the authority for the guardian to act.

Each state will have their own guidelines for the authorities and restrictions of a guardian. In Oregon, the powers and duties of a guardian are defined in ORS 125.315.

Powers and Duties

- The guardian has custody of the protected person and may establish the protected person's place of abode within or without this state.
- The guardian shall provide for the care, comfort and maintenance of the protected person and, whenever appropriate, shall arrange for training and education of the protected person. Without regard to custodial rights of the protected person, the guardian shall take reasonable care of the person's clothing, furniture and other personal effects unless a conservator has been appointed for the protected person.
- The guardian may consent, refuse consent or withhold or withdraw consent to health care for the protected person.

The guardian may:
- Make advance funeral and burial arrangements;
- Control the disposition of the remains of the protected person; and
- Make an anatomical gift of all or any part of the body of the protected person.
- The guardian of a minor has the powers and responsibilities of a parent who has legal custody of a child, except that the guardian has no obligation to support the minor beyond the support that can be provided from the estate of the minor, and the guardian is not liable for the torts of the minor. The guardian may consent to the marriage or adoption of a protected person who is a minor.
- The guardian may receive money and personal property deliverable to the protected person and apply the money and property for support, care and education of the protected person. The guardian shall exercise care to conserve any excess for the protected person's needs.
- If a conservator has been appointed for the protected person, the guardian may file a motion with the court seeking an order of the court on the duties of the conservator relating to payment of support for the protected person.
- A guardian may consent to the withholding or withdrawing of artificially administered nutrition and hydration for a protected person only under certain circumstances described in Oregon law, and

if the protected person has a certain medical condition specified in Oregon law.

Limitations

- A guardian may not authorize the sterilization of the protected person.
- A guardian may not use funds from the protected person's estate for room and board that the guardian or guardian's spouse, parent or child have furnished the protected person unless the charge for the service is approved by order of the court _before_ the payment is made.
- Before a guardian may place an adult protected person in a mental health treatment facility, a nursing home or other residential facility, the guardian must file a statement with the court informing the court that the guardian intends to make the placement.
- Notice of the statement of intent must be given to interested parties. In addition, notice of the statement of intent to move must be given by the guardian to the following persons:

    1. Any attorney who represented the protected person at any time during the protective proceeding.
    2. If the protected person is a resident of a nursing home or residential facility, or if the notice states the intention to place the protected person in a nursing home or residential facility, the office of the Long Term Care Ombudsman.

- If the protected person is a resident of a mental health treatment facility or a residential facility for individuals with developmental disabilities, or if the notice states the intention to place the protected person in such a facility, the notice given to the protected person must clearly indicate the manner in which the protected person may object to the proposed placement.
- The guardian may thereafter place the adult protected person in a mental health treatment facility, a nursing home or other residential facility without further court order. If an objection is made, the court shall schedule a hearing on the objection as soon as practicable.

Acquiring the Case

One of the first acts of the guardian when acquiring a case is to assess the current placement and situation of the protected person and insure they are safe. The guardian needs to meet with the protected person, family members, and the doctors and medical practitioners involved with the care and treatment of the protected person. The guardian needs to understand the medical situation, the protected person's abilities and limitations and create a care plan for the protected person. If the situation requires immediate intervention, the guardian needs to locate the appropriate placement for the protected person and contact the court immediately with the intent to move.

All of this needs to be done within days of the appointment. Often, the person will be in a safe environment if minor changes are made to their immediate care. Maybe companions need to be brought into the home to assist with the administration of medicines, or preparing meals, or just insuring the protected person is safe. The guardian needs to quickly assess the situation and take immediate action if warranted. Most family or friend appointed guardianships are done with the agreement of family members and is not a contentious or dangerous case to acquire.

Or, you could be appointed as guardian in a dangerous situation. I explained earlier about a case where law authorities converged on a house and removed the threat, leaving a demented, elderly woman in confusion with no safe place to stay. We had to quickly assess the threat, locate a facility that could keep her safe, and move her there with doctor's orders.....in a few hours, after we received the emergency guardianship appointment.

Once the guardian is confident that the protected person is safe, the guardian needs to gather a mountain of information to create a care plan.

Knowing the Person

The guardian needs to fully understand who the protected person is. As a family member or friend, you should have much of your knowledge about the respondent because of your personal connection. This will assist you with creating a care plan that provides as much self-determination in a least restrictive environment as possible.

If not, then the guardian should meet with the protected person at length and, if the protected person is able to express themselves, inquire as much as is possible about what their preferences are. Below is partial list of topics that the guardian should inquire about.

- Religious preference
- Hobbies
- Skills
- Entertainment
- Education
- Interests
- History
- Family
- Estate plan
- Political preference
- Food preferences/diet
- Treatment
- Resuscitation
- Life support
- Burial
- Anatomical donation

Once the guardian has met with the person, they should meet with family members, doctors and care staff to continue to add to their knowledge of the protected person and their care needs. Thorough investigation will enable the guardian to better understand who the person is and develop an appropriate care plan suitable to the person.

Case Study – We once were appointed guardian for an elderly woman who was quite demented and in a facility. She was unable to express herself verbally, but was communicative through expressions and actions. It was easy to see when she was happy, sad, or angry. We heard from staff that she wanted to go to the park each week with a packed lunch of peanut butter and jelly sandwiches, and feed the ducks. The staff had been arranging her weekly trip for years, but no one really knew why. All they knew was that on Thursdays the lady was ready to go and became irritated if they did not leave by noon, rain or shine.

We continued the process without knowing why. As we acquired the case, we met with family members and medical staff. One of the distant family members was able to shed some light on why the woman had this routine.

Apparently, the protected person was married for many years. Her husband passed away some twenty years prior. During their marriage, they began a routine in their senior years of them going to the park on Thursdays for a picnic lunch. They would feed the ducks and then walk around the park together. It was a simple routine. We never understood why it had to be Thursdays, but we totally understood the significance of the picnic lunch and feeding the ducks. We continued that routine until she was unable to leave the facility due to her medical condition. She passed away soon after.

Everyone has a story, and the story often gets lost in time. Researching and understanding the protected person will undoubtedly reveal many interesting, lost stories.

Many states require that the guardian conduct regular, monthly visits to insure their protected person is getting the proper care. During your visits, you should read the chart notes, meet with attending doctors, nurses and staff. You could physically inspect the person for bruises, sores, or lesions if appropriate. The appearance of any of these could indicate either physical abuse or inadequate care. Usually, interviews and reading chart notes is sufficient.

Case Study – My wife started her career in the public conservator's office in Sacramento, California. She was a new public conservator case manager and was assigned to visit many of the protected persons on the county caseload to insure the persons were receiving proper care. Several of her cases required her to meet with a lady who ran a foster home. Her name was Dorthea Puente.

Dorthea was an elderly lady herself. She had several residents in her large, Victorian home in downtown Sacramento. My wife recalls meeting her on several occasions to discuss the county's cases. Dorthea was pleasant and seemed to be providing very good care to the persons in my wife's caseload.

The only problem was....she was a murderer.

A news story broke that Dorthea was arrested for the murder of nine to 15 residents who lived in her foster home. She would murder the residents and bury them in the basement or backyard or put them in a large box and nail it shut. She would have someone dump the boxes with their bodies in rural areas under the guise it was garbage or junk in the box. Dorthea would continue to collect their social security or other benefits payments. After some inquiries by family members and an investigation conducted, seven bodies were recovered. She was eventually charged with nine murders, convicted of three, and sentenced to life in prison where she died.

And to think my wife had lunch with her on several occasions.

It is important to visit your protected person and make sure they are safe. Even more important, make sure they are still alive. Sounds crazy, but with people like Dorthea Puente out there, one never knows......

Care Plan

A care plan for a protected person should be created by the guardian immediately after appointment. The care plan should be created with the intent of providing the least restrictive means of care while promoting the most amount of self-determination possible. The information gathered by the guardian from varying parties and personal observations will contribute to the development of the care plan.

Medical/Placement - The guardian needs to completely understand the medical condition of their ward in order to properly place the person in the appropriate facility. They need to fully know the diagnosis, prognosis, and current treatment options for the ward. This will create the basis of the care plan.

If at all possible, the guardian should gather information that would reveal trends or baseline comparatives to help determine the best level of care for the protected person. A person could have several mini mental evaluations over a period of time, showing a deterioration in the person's cognitive abilities. This would suggest that the proper placement for this person would eventually be a memory care facility up to the level of a secured ward. Or, a person could show declining mobility, suggesting the protected person needed a facility where decreased mobility can be met with increased attention by the employees or caregivers. Comparative analysis of medical trends can provide valuable information to the guardian to make the best choice of care for the protected person.

The guardian should heed the recommendations of the protected person's medical practitioners and ask them for their opinion. They can add tremendous value to understanding the level of care the protected person requires, and what the guardian can expect for future care needs.

The guardian might also choose to have a third party assessment conducted by an independent party, such as another professional fiduciary or medical practitioner. An assessment is a formal evaluation of the needs of a person, be it financial, medical, or care. A third party assessment will gather information for the guardian to make the best decision possible for the protected person's care and placement.

Caregivers/Companions

As guardian or conservator, you will likely find yourself in a position where you have to hire someone to provide some level of care for your protected person. This can be a companion who helps take the person shopping and to appointments, or a caregiver; someone who provides specific care for the person. In either case, there are some considerations for the fiduciary.

Caregiving Company – There are a myriad of professional caregiving companies sprouting up all over the area. These companies have employees that they hire to provide care to persons. You, as the guardian or conservator, could hire the company to provide care to your ward. The care company would conduct a visit and interview to see what level of care the person is at and charge accordingly. They would discuss specific care requests that you have and create a schedule of services. They would have all of the documents that the caregiver would need to complete while providing care, such as care notes, diet observation, transportation schedules, medicine administration lists, and so on.

The care company will vet the caregiver for you. They conduct background checks to make sure the person is not a criminal. You, as the fiduciary, hire the caregiving company and they supply the caregiver. This greatly reduces your liability as fiduciary should something go wrong.

The positive side of hiring a company is that you have a large resource to draw from for providing care. They can provide someone for any day or time and add people as needed.

The downside is the cost is relatively high. It can run $17,000 to $20,000 a month for full-time, in home care, depending on the level of care needed. Another downside is that the caregiver can change from day to day resulting in inconsistency of care. Elderly persons, particularly those with cognitive impairment like dementia, do not accept change well. The more stable and consistent the care is, the better for the protected person.

Independent Contractors – There are many people who provide companion or caregiving who are self-employed, thus independent contractors. You, as fiduciary, need to make sure these are truly contractors and operate as such. It is easy for them to claim they work for your company rather than independently. Here are some guidelines;

- The contractor should have a business license or DBA (doing business as) account at a bank.
- The contractor should have an agreement or contract with you explaining the nature of their services and estimated costs.
- The contractor needs to direct their own details of their work and schedule. You, as fiduciary, should provide the basic structure of the care; transportation to medical appointments, prepare meals, clean,

assist with ADL (activities of daily living like bathing, toilet, etc), prepare medicine trays, etc. The contractor decides when and how to do these tasks. You give general directions, they work out the details.

- The contractor should still provide a background check for you.
- The contractor should submit their invoice for services.
- The contractor should provide a daily narrative of the condition of the ward, meals, and activities/behaviors observed.

Be sure to clarify with the person that they are a contractor and not an employee. If there is any question or confusion, don't hire them. Always check with your attorney first.

Domestic Employees – Another option is to hire domestic employees to provide care. The estate can be set up as the employer to hire people to be employees to provide care. In this arrangement, the fiduciary directs every aspect of the employee's job. The fiduciary sets the schedules, provides the documents to complete, performs employee background checks, obtains worker's compensation insurance, receives timesheets, processes payroll and withholds employee taxes. This is no different than if the caregiver went to work for a company providing caregiving service. The only difference is that the estate of the protected person is the employer.

The downside to this is trying to find the right people to provide the care. You're not limited to use just contractors, but can use anyone. Family members or friends can be used, but should be disclosed to the court to avoid a perceived conflict of interest.

The upside is the costs to the estate are considerably less than using a company to provide the caregivers. We pay an average of $8,000 to $12,000 a month for full-time, in-home care for a person using employees of the estate. Plus, you can create consistency of care by having the same caregiver report to provide care to the same person.

Make sure that anyway you decide to go, you have a good plan and good caregivers in place. Be clear with your expectations, follow up with the caregivers, and provide feedback to improve their performance. If issues develop, address them immediately.

Medicaid

Often, a person under guardianship will have increased care costs as their conditions continue or worsen. The care can be at home or in a facility. If the person has limited funds combined with significant care needs, the guardian should consider how long the funds will last at the current expense rate and when the person will likely need Medicaid coverage.

Medicaid is a state funded resource that provides medical care for persons with limited assets and income. Medicaid also pays for the facility for a person to be housed in, such as assisted living or nursing home. If the person's estate is large enough, then a trustee or conservator might be appointed. In any case, the guardian needs to understand the nature of the person's estate and create a Medicaid spend-down plan in conjunction with a care plan.

Some facilities are not Medicaid approved. Some are. The guardian should seek Medicaid facilities that will allow a person to private pay and spend down to Medicaid levels. This will assure the guardian, the protected person and interested parties that the protected person will be cared for as their medical condition worsens and they need to go on Medicaid *without having to move*. This is extremely important. Consistency of care and placement adds significant stability to the case and the protected person.

Many facilities will not take new residents unless they have had a period of time where they pay privately before they go on Medicaid. The guardian should research which facilities are Medicaid appropriate and what their requirements are for accepting new residents.

Limited Guardianship

In some instances, a limited guardianship might be appropriate to protect a vulnerable person. This is when the scope of authority of the guardian is limited, not the duration. It is much like a limited conservatorship. For example, a person could be found mentally incapacitated, but has a healthcare representative appointed. The person might be going through a divorce, and needs a guardian to execute the terms of divorce, but not the healthcare. Or an incapacitated person might be in the hospital and needs to be relocated to a lower level of care on hospice. The family objects and the hospital files for a limited guardianship to decide if the person should be moved. In each of these situations, the court would need to review the petition, review the evidence, review the capacity of the protected person, hear from each party in a hearing, and rule on the appropriateness of a limited guardianship.

Once the action has been completed, the guardian files a report with the court and petitions to terminate the guardianship.

Temporary Guardianship

Sometimes a temporary, or emergency, guardianship is appropriate for a certain situation. When a person is at risk of immediate injury or death to themselves or others, a temporary guardianship can be appointed to take control of the situation, protect the person, and determine if a continued guardianship should be sought. The purpose of the temporary is spelled out in the petition and ruled by the court.

Case Study 1 – We were contacted by Adult Protective Service because an elderly lady was found by neighbors laying in her driveway in the snow wearing a nightgown. The woman was transported to the hospital for treatment, but the hospital did not know who to contact and the woman was severely demented and unable to communicate her wishes. APS investigated the situation and discovered the elderly woman was living at home with her adult son, who was supposed to be the caregiver. The son had convictions for drug crimes and was not watching his mother as he should and was absent. APS also discovered the woman had a daughter in another state. We contacted the daughter with APS, explained the situation, and the daughter asked us to petition to be the temporary guardian to protect the woman and have her treated.

The daughter authorized immediate treatment for her mother.

We were appointed temporary guardian in a few days, assessed the situation, and petitioned to become the permanent guardian because of the neglect of the adult son. We soon transferred the woman to a facility and continued to oversee her care for several years.

The adult son, who was in his mid-forties, died from a heart attack within a couple of years after our appointment.

Case Study 2 – We received a call from Adult Protective Services in a distant county. Apparently, a husband and wife went to a grocery store to shop. The husband went into the store and the wife stayed in the car. She was Japanese and had a difficult time with the English language, though she had lived in this country for years. She also suffered from dementia.

The husband had a heart attack in the store and was transported to the hospital. The wife wandered into the store six hours later looking for her husband. The store staff was able to figure out that her husband was the one transported to the hospital. They called Adult Protective Services who contacted us.

We met with the wife the next morning at her house with the APS worker. Her husband was severely ill and in the hospital. The couple had no local relatives and no children. APS asked us to petition for an emergency guardianship. By the end of the day, the court issued the temporary letters of guardianship and conservatorship. We were able to secure funds from the woman's account, hire 24-hour in-home caregivers, and assure she was safe before the day ended.

The woman's husband passed away and we were appointed as conservator and guardian for the woman.

Disabilities

Most of the cases we have been appointed on over the years have fallen into these three categories; Dementia/Mental Illness/Developmentally Disabled. Each area has its unique challenges to managing the person. Yes, every case and every person is different, but we have seen many similarities over the years in each of these categories. To give you a better understanding of the challenges to managing each type of disability under guardianship, I thought I would give you a few case studies.

Dementia – There are many types of dementia. Dementia is a broad category of brain diseases that cause a long-term and often gradual decrease in the ability to think and remember that is great enough to affect a person's daily functioning. It is a deterioration of cognitive ability and memory loss. It can easily lead to dysfunctional behaviors, unmanageable persons, wandering, and the likes. The most feared type of dementia is Alzheimer's.

Dementia, in particular Alzheimer's, can require periodic assistance when first diagnosed. Many people with dementia need assistance with their activities of daily living (ADL), such as bathing, cooking, medicine management, shopping, bill paying, and so on. As the disease progresses, the caregiving and costs increase until the person likely requires 24-hour continuous care.

Case Study – We have several clients that suffer from early onset Alzheimer's. One woman was 55 years old when she was diagnosed and able to communicate well and was high functioning. At 57 she had difficulties remembering how to cook or when to take her medicines. She still conversed, went to baseball games, laughed, played with her children, and liked to go for walks. The husband provided caregiving on a periodic basis, but was getting burned out.

At 58 she was unable to count money, change the television channels, or prepare a sandwich. She needed assistance with dressing. She was having small toileting accidents. Her husband tried to get her to move to a facility, but it didn't work out. The woman had a large enough estate to pay for her care in her home. The woman had a daily caregiver for eight hours a day. The husband moved out.

At 60 she could hardly remember her two children. She was unable to talk much and communicated mostly with chuckles and smiles. She was unable to dress herself. She needed assistance with bathing and toileting. She was incontinent of bowl and bladder, she could not leave the house without someone with her. She began to wander. She required 24-hour onsite caregiving in her home. Her spouse filed for divorce.

At 62 she was unable to communicate, feed herself, bathe, take medicines, cook, dress, or toilet. She didn't recognize her children through pictures or respond when asked about them. She would sit on the sofa and watch television, occasionally laughing or chuckling at odd scenes. She had 24-hour in-home caregiving. She had a large estate and was able to stay in her home.

Dementia can be subtle or severe. In this case, the protected person had an estate sufficient to support 24-hour in-home care at a cost of $15,000+ per month. Most other persons with smaller estates would have been directed to move into a memory care facility when they were unable to cook, dress, and began to wander.

Other forms of dementia may not progress as quickly, but the ultimate outcome is the same for most all persons. Developing a care plan must include increased cost of care as the dementia progresses.

Developmentally Disabled/Brain Injury – These types of cases require a detailed assessment of the protected person and the probability of some rehabilitation or education to improve their quality of life. A person who is developmentally disabled can be very high functioning. We have several cases where a developmentally disabled person is able to hold down a job (janitor/cleaning) and live in an apartment with little oversight. A conservator manages the funds while the person manages most of their daily activities. If a guardian is appointed, they should determine the least amount of intervention to allow for the most amount of self-determination and independence possible.

Case Study – My wife was managing a case more than twenty years ago caring for a developmentally disabled couple. When we were appointed as conservator for them, they were married and living in a car. The man was illiterate, the woman disabled. Over the years, my wife discovered that there was a supplemental needs trust managed by an out-of-state sister. My wife got the couple on Social Security Disability, discovered a small pension for the husband for janitorial work years prior, and worked with the trustee to receive and manage funds for the sister.

Today, they are living in their own manufactured home, drive a little car around town, go on vacations, garden, and visit with us at the office regularly.

Mentally Ill – Managing the care of a mentally ill person can be, by far, the most challenging task for a guardian. Mental illness is still very much an unknown field. Yes, we know a lot about chemical imbalances, medicines that work for various diagnosis, and holistic approaches to diet and mental illness, but the fact is that a person who is mentally ill can be extremely volatile, unpredictable and difficult to manage. To give you an idea, I have a case study that is an excellent example of what can go wrong.

Case Study - Sandy was a morbidly obese, 48 year-old woman who was mentally ill and had one leg. She suffered with schizophrenia and bi-polar disorders. Experts also believed she was developmentally disabled, but there were to records to substantiate it. She often had outbursts that resulted in assaults against the closest person. She was in a wheel chair, but had a prosthetic leg. Sandy was in jail and homeless when we first met her. She would ride the local bus, get mad at someone, take off her leg and beat them with it. Then, she would go to jail. After a day in jail, she would be discharged to the hospital. After a few hours, staff at the hospital would clean her up and send her back to the streets without admitting her. They had no place to discharge her to, other than the state hospital, which was full. Sandy would repeat the cycle over and over and over again.

We were contacted by county mental health who asked us to be her guardian under contract with them. The goal was to get her to a level of care appropriate for her and to try and get some treatment for her. We agreed and, after a great deal of time and effort, Sandy was finally admitted to the state hospital for two years. She was discharged to a foster home that was specially built by the county for her and other violent, mentally ill patients where she stayed for almost ten years. We were her guardian the entire time.

Then it happened.

Sandy was evicted for violent outbursts and threats against the staff. Sandy had done this before and there was no consequence. What was different this time is that one of the owners of the foster home was pregnant and concerned for the welfare of her unborn child. Also, the facility was tired of her outbursts and assaults and decided they had enough. She was evicted.

Over the course of the next three months, our staff spent more than _400 hours_ trying to manage her case. We had calls every day, all day and night, for months. Sandy went through every motel and hotel in the county and was eventually refused rooms everywhere. She became homeless. We tried foster homes, facilities, hospitals, in and out of the area with no luck.

We continued to get her medicines to her each day along with a bag of food and some limited funds for her spending. We made sure she had clothes, a sleeping bag, cigarettes and blankets. This went on for weeks. Occasionally she would get into a motel and get cleaned up with the help of a companion we could find. Then, after two or three days, she would be evicted and banned from the motel for unruly or assaultive.

One early morning we received an emergency call at 2:00 A.M. from the police. Sandy was again evicted from a motel for assaulting a guest. The policeman on the phone asked if we were the guardian. We acknowledged we were. He said he was going to file charges against us for elder abuse because we were abandoning the vulnerable, disabled person. We tried to explain the situation, but he wanted us to personally drive there, pick her up, and take her home with us to care for her. We told him we would not do that. We said she should go to the hospital for an evaluation.

He said he was going to file elder abuse charges against my wife as guardian. Two weeks later, we discovered that he had not followed through with his threats.

Sandy continued to cycle in and out of the system. She had an emergency and went to the emergency room. We were able to talk them into admitting her into the hospital. During her stay, we obtained school records to prove she was developmentally disabled. She was scheduled to go to a developmentally *disabled foster home, but suffered a heart attack and stroke and died before she was placed.*

This is a tragic case. As the guardian, our responsibility was to try and manage her care; <u>not personally provide it</u>. The issue with being a guardian for a mentally ill person is that they can, and likely will, be non-compliant and unpredictable. Most states will not allow forced medications. That means you can expect erratic behaviors, non-compliance, and lots of chaos on a case like this.

Be very, very careful of becoming a guardian for a mentally ill person. It is a daunting task that can quickly become a real nightmare for a very long time.

The Decision Making Process

The National Guardianship Association (NGA) has detailed the Standards of Practice for professional fiduciaries. I believe these standards should apply to laymen guardians, be they family members or friends. Much of their documentation and recommendations refer to the appointment of a person as a guardian. The following information comes from the NGA Standards of Practice with my commentary and examples.

There are three issues of making a decision regarding treatment or management of the guardianship. Informed consent, substituted judgment, and best interest.

Informed consent

Informed Consent is the guardian's agreement to a particular course of action based on a full disclosure of the facts needed to make the decision intelligently. The guardian stands in the place of the protected person and is entitled to the same information and freedom of choice as the protected person would have received if he or she were not under guardianship. In evaluating each decision, the guardian shall do the following:

- Have a clear understanding of the issue for which informed consent is being sought.

- Have a clear understanding of the options, expected outcomes, risks and benefits of each alternative.
- Determine the conditions that necessitate treatment or action.
- Encourage and support the protected person in understanding the facts and directing a decision.
- Maximize the participation of the protected person in making the decision.
- Determine whether the protected person has previously stated preferences in regard to a decision of this nature.
- Determine why this decision needs to be made now rather than Later.
- Determine what will happen if a decision is made to take no action.
- Determine what the least restrictive alternative is for this situation.
- Obtain a second medical or professional opinion, if necessary.
- Obtain information or input from family and from other professionals.
- Obtain written documentation of all reports relevant to each decision.

Once this information has been gathered and assessed, the guardian should make the decision that the protected person would have made if they had the choice. This is called substituted judgment.

Substituted judgment

Substituted judgment is the principle of decision-making that substitutes the decision the protected person would have made when the person had capacity as the guiding force in any surrogate decision the guardian makes. Sometimes the substituted judgement decision will conflict with the guardian's personal values or beliefs. It is important for the guardian to understand they should ***never*** impose their personal values or beliefs on the protected person. They are there for the protected person and no one else.

Substituted judgment promotes the underlying values of self-determination and the well-being of the protected person. It is not used when the wishes would cause substantial harm to the protected person or when the guardian cannot establish the protected person's goals or preferences even with support.

First, the guardian shall ask the protected person what he or she wants. This may sound simple, but the guardian can easily fall into the trap that the person is not competent or unable to communicate.

Second, if the protected person has difficulty expressing what he or she wants, the guardian shall do everything possible to help the protected person express his or her goals, needs, and preferences. Only when the protected person, even with assistance, cannot express his or her goals and preferences, shall the guardian seek input from others familiar with the protected person to determine what the individual would have wanted.

Case study – We had a woman under guardianship who had a series of strokes that left her unable to speak, gesture, or communicate in any normal fashion. She would occasionally smile, but there were virtually no emotions or signs that she could communicate her wishes. Most people thought she was completely comatose and unable to communicate at all.

What we discovered through trial and error was that she could communicate through blinking. One blink was a yes. Two blinks was a no. Through a series of yes and no questions, we were able to determine much of her wishes and desires, not just for treatment and medical decisions, but for life actions in general. At one point, she was molested in a facility and using the communication process through blinking, we determined who the perpetrator was and what happened from her perspective. The perpetrator eventually pled guilty and was sentenced to five years in prison.

Best Interest

Finally, only when the protected person's goals and preferences cannot be ascertained even with support, or when following the protected person's wishes would result in substantial harm, then the guardian may make a decision based in the person's best interest based on the information that the guardian as obtained. The Best Interest principle requires that the guardian consider the least intrusive, most normalizing and least restrictive course of action possible to provide for the needs of the protected person. The guardian still needs to consider past practice and reliable source information of likely choices.

The decision making process for a guardian is not simple, and requires a great deal of time, patience, ingenuity, and determination. It is your responsibility as a guardian to seek the best solution for the protected person that they would have made if able to, or to make the best decision based on the information you have. Above all else, be sure to document every action and the information you obtained to make a decision.

Funeral and burial

One of the first acts of the guardian after appointment is to review and make end of life plans for the protected person. The guardian needs to arrange funeral, burial, and disposition of remains for the protected person if no plans exist. The same process for exercising substituted judgment should be executed here to obtain the prepaid burial plan arrangements that the protected person would have wanted based on the information the guardian obtains.

The guardian needs to consider the religious preferences of the protected person. The guardian needs to investigate the wishes of the protected person through interviews with family members and friends. The guardian needs to decide the burial and funeral arrangements and the disposition of remains of the protected person. The disposition of remains is a critical piece of the burial and funeral arrangements. We have had family members or friends become extremely upset when it came to the disposition of remains. Great care must be given to thoroughly research the preferences of the protected person before making the decision. On occasion, the guardian should communicate their decision to involved parties to provide them an opportunity to object or voice their opinion. If the parties continue to be contentious toward the decision, the guardian may choose to petition the court for instructions and provide the evidence to support their decision. The court would make the final ruling.

The guardian may have to dispose of the personal property of the protected person if no estate plan is in place. The guardian may need to open probate or a small estate (see the chapter on Personal Representatives/Executors) to dispose of the personal property.

Termination of the Guardianship

The guardianship terminates when the court issues an order terminating the guardianship. This will occur after the protected person's burial and funeral arrangements are completed, the disposition of remains has been completed, and the personal property disposed of. A final report of the guardian is submitted to the court along with a petition to close the guardianship.

A guardianship can also be terminated when the protected person regains capacity. This may seem far-fetched, but in the case of a brain injury, mental illness, or other cognitive impairment that could be reversed, a guardianship could be terminated and the protected person regain their rights for self-determination.

Case Study – We were appointed guardian for a woman who was severely mentally ill. When my wife went to the farm to meet with the respondent and the companion, she was shocked at what she saw. The front door to the house was partially open. My wife called as she knocked and slowly pushed the door open. The respondent was standing behind a kitchen counter wearing nothing but a bloody t-shirt. She had a cleaver in her hand and was cutting up chicken pieces and throwing the body parts against the kitchen wall near the sink. When she saw my wife peek in, she threw a chicken body part at her that hit the door and splattered blood.

My wife was so shocked that she ran out the front door. She realized she had not seen the companion, so she started searching the property. She continued to call the companion's name as she ran through the horse arena and horse stalls, hoping she was there somewhere. The companion soon called back and asked what was wrong. My wife was terribly relieved and explained the situation. They went back to the house, cleaned up the woman and the kitchen, and began the interview for the guardianship.

We took the case and were appointed the guardian for the chicken lady. After three years of intensive oversight, proper medications, thorough training and follow up, the protected person, aka chicken lady, was released from the guardianship. We petitioned the court to terminate the guardianship because the woman had regained her capacity. She told my wife at the hearing, "I've been in a fog for years, and I don't remember much. All I can say is thank you for giving me my life back."

The woman went on to enroll in classes at the college and live independently.

Guardianships can be terminated for good cause.

Annual Guardianship Report

A guardian is required to file an annual guardian's report with the court. The guardian's report will vary from state to state, but many will contain the same information on the case.

- Explain the overall medical condition, impairment, social and physical condition of the protected person.
- List the address and type of all living arrangements and places where the protected person lived during the reporting period, including the dates when each stay began or ended.
- Explain whether you believe the current living situation is in the protected person's best interest.
- Describe the medical, educational, vocational, and social services provided to the protected person during the period.
- Give your opinion about the adequacy of the care provided.
- Explain the medication the protected person was prescribed during the reporting period. Attach a list of medicines.
- Describe the nature and frequency of visits by you or family members with the protected person during the reporting period.
- Describe the extent that the protected person was able to participate in the decision making process.
- Rate the level of care the protected person received during the reporting period.
- Describe the needs of the protected person for continued guardianship and recommendations for changes to the guardianship or future care of the protected person.

- Describe the residences, level of care, and services you plan for the protected person for the next 18 months.
- Complete the summary of financial activity of you managed the funds of the protected person during the reporting period.

The annual guardianship report should provide enough information to the court to explain what has happened during the year, if any progress is made, and what the future plans are for the protected person and the guardianship. Be sure to provide as much information as possible to satisfy the court's inquiry about the protected person and the guardianship.

Personal Property/Finances

If there is no fiduciary managing the personal property or finances of the protected person, then the guardian may receive authority from the court to do so. The guardian would go through many of the same steps as a conservator to control, inventory, and manage the finances and personal property of the protected person. We suggest guardians use the same format as a conservator to report the annual accounting to the court along with the guardianship.

At the time of death of the protected person, the guardian would turn the assets of the estate over to the personal representative if a will is in place, or to the trustee if a pour over will is in place.

Consideration for Guardians

The appointment of a guardian is significant. As guardian, you take over every aspect of a person's health, medical care, and well-being. It is usually an appointment for the remainder of their lives.

Be aware that taking on a case involving a mentally ill person can be chaotic, challenging, unpredictable, and very difficult to manage.

Take careful consideration of every decision you make. Know your protected person. Know the resources available to you. Plan the care carefully and adjust regularly.

Chapter 7
Healthcare Representative

A healthcare representative (or healthcare power or attorney) is appointed by a person to make healthcare decisions on behalf of the person, known as the principal, if the principal becomes incapable or incapacitated. Normally, the appointment of a healthcare representative is performed when the principal completes their advanced directives, which are a set of instructions, wishes, and desires regarding healthcare that are recorded by the principal for future reference. The advanced directives includes a section which is a power of attorney appointment for healthcare.

A healthcare representative can be appointed in most, if not all, states. A capable adult may designate in writing a competent adult to serve as a healthcare representative. A capable adult may also designate a competent adult to serve as an alternative healthcare representative if the original designee is unavailable, unable or unwilling to serve any time after the healthcare power of attorney is executed. The healthcare power of attorney is effective when it is signed, witnessed and accepted as required by law.

Any capable adult may execute a healthcare instruction, or advanced directive. A person who has been determined to be incapable, or lacks capacity, cannot execute the appointment of a healthcare representative through the power of attorney in the advanced directive. A guardianship would be appropriate to provide for the healthcare needs of such a person.

The appointment shall be effective when the healthcare power of attorney is signed and witnessed as required by law.

Unless the period of time that an advance directive is to be effective is limited by the terms of the advance directive, the advance directive shall continue in effect until:
- The principal dies; or
- The advance directive is revoked, suspended or superseded pursuant to law.

If the principal is incapable at the expiration of the term of the advance directive, the advance directive continues in effect until:

- The principal is no longer incapable;
- The principal dies; or
- The advance directive is revoked, suspended or superseded pursuant to the provisions of law.

A healthcare provider shall make a copy of an advance directive and any other instrument a part of the principal's medical record when a copy of that instrument is provided to the principal's healthcare provider.

The healthcare representative stands in the place of the principal when the principal is incapacitated and makes medical and care decisions on behalf of the principal. The decisions can include;

- Life sustaining treatment
- Administration of antibiotics
- Blood transfusions
- Resuscitation/non resuscitation
- Life support systems
- Amputations
- Sterilizations
- Medicine administrations

Any medical care that a person could encounter can be decided by the healthcare representative. This is exactly the same as a guardianship, except there is no court oversight, no annual report to the court or interested parties, no real accountability. It is a significant appointment that should be well considered before a person is appointed or accepts as the appointee.

If a healthcare representative is appointed by an individual, then a guardianship is normally not required or needed. Sometimes the court will revoke a healthcare representative when a guardianship is appointed. However, in our years of serving as both, I have only seen that done one time, and it involved a case of elder abuse by the healthcare representative.

A copy of the healthcare representative appointment should be filed with all medical practitioners involved with the care of the principal. It would behoove the appointed healthcare representative to have a copy of their appointment ready if they need to accompany a principal to a medical appointment or sign for medical treatment. A healthcare representative has full access to all medical information regarding the principal as if the principal was seeking the information.

The healthcare representative can use the advanced directives as a guide for making medical and treatment decisions. They should also gather as much information as possible, similar to a guardian, to insure they can make substituted judgment decisions on behalf of the principal.

Not all persons can be appointed as a healthcare representative. Oregon law prohibits appointees for a variety of reasons. The following persons may not serve as health care representatives in Oregon:

- Someone unrelated to the principal by blood, marriage or adoption, except by court order, if they are one of the following;
    - The attending physician or an employee of the attending physician; or
    - An owner, operator or employee of a health care facility in which the principal is a patient or resident, unless the health care representative was appointed before the principal's admission to the facility.
    - A person who is the principal's parent or former guardian and at any time while the principal was under the care, custody or control of the person, a court entered an order intervening in the oversight and care of the principal for a variety of reasons, such as abuse, safety, etc.
    - A person who is appointed but has been disqualified or removed from a prior appointment as a healthcare representative or care provider.

Each state has their own laws to determine who is and is not appropriate to be appointed as a healthcare representative. Read the laws of your state regarding healthcare representative appointments or consult with an atorney before you decide to be appointed for someone.

Chapter 8
Advanced Directives

Advanced directives are a series of detailed instructions that a capable, or competent, person completes explaining what treatments and care preferences they have for themselves. The document usually has no expiration date, but can be revoked at any time.

The advanced directives cover a myriad of treatment directives for serious medical situations. The directives focus on end-of-life care.

For example, if the person is close to death, do they want tube feeding or life support? Is that to be the decision of the representative, or will the decision be based on the doctor's recommendations? If a person is permanently unconscious, such as in a coma, do they want tube feeding or life support? If a person has advanced progressive illness where they can no longer swallow, care for themselves, communicate, or recognize their family, do they want tube feeding or life support? If a person has extraordinary suffering and any treatment would prolong their pain, would they want tube feeding or life support?

These are serious questions that should be addressed and discussed between the principal and their healthcare representative. The principal has opportunities to add language to clarify their wishes in several places in the document. Some directives address the issue of antibiotics. It is important to understand what this document addresses and what the wishes of the principal are. For example, a person might not want life support if the chances of their survival is less than 50%; or 25%. Maybe there is a miracle drug that just came out that could improve their chances. Maybe a blood transfusion could cure them, but their religious beliefs forbid any such action regardless of the benefit.

A principal must understand the significance of the document that they are completing, and the healthcare representative must also understand the desires and wishes of the principal. This takes a lot of time and communication at the time the document is being completed and the appointment made.

Chapter 9
Case Management Assistance by a
Professional Fiduciary

There are times when the expertise of a professional fiduciary is sought without the appointment through a document (such as a power of attorney) or a court. Professional fiduciaries gain a wealth of knowledge as they mature in their field of expertise. Other persons, mostly family members, who have been appointed as a fiduciary through an estate planning document, such as a will or trust, can find themselves in a position that is new, foreign, and quite challenging. They might be in a different location than the estate or the person. They might have their own challenges and don't have the time, skills, or desire to work in the appointed capacity. Becoming a fiduciary for someone may not be on the relative's radar and usually comes as a surprise or burden.

There are also those persons who have cared for a loved one for many years. It might start out as a benign relationship of a daughter helping out mom and dad with some shopping or bill paying once a week. As the person's care needs increase, the time and effort increases. Eventually, the care needs increase to the point the daughter or loved one transitions from a daughter to a caregiver, spending the majority of their time providing care and neglecting their personal life. This is tragically true if the elderly person has developed Alzheimer's or other form of dementia.

These persons need help, but not necessarily a fiduciary, to manage the case. A case manager is someone who can help coordinate services through the contacts that they have already vetted. Over the years, our company has used hundreds of persons, private caregivers, contractors and the like to provide services to our clients. As a case manager, we can utilize our knowledge of managing a case combined with our list of vetted resources to help another fiduciary manage their case. This is done under a simple agreement between you as a representative of the estate, and a professional fiduciary.

Services/Case Study

A person can be appointed as healthcare representative, trustee or power of attorney and be in a different location. They could have a situation where their loved one has become incapacitated through a medical condition or an event, such as a stroke or fall. As a case manager, the professional can work with the fiduciary to manage the care and finances for the person. Through delegated authority and release of information forms, they can assist with coordinating many of the services that the person needs.

- Transportation to medical appointments
- Managing in-home caregivers
- Coordinating home repairs or maintenance
- Medicine management
- Financial management/bill paying
- Discharge from the hospital
- Rehabilitation
- Home sale
- Moves
- Inventory/insurance
- Protection of the person

Presenting this information as a professional fiduciary, when we work with a distant fiduciary, we prefer to have access to funds that will enable us to make low level decisions and pay for services. We do that by creating a company trust account for the benefit of the person. It is a separate account that we manage for the person. The distant fiduciary transfers funds into the new account for us to manage. We then use the funds as agreed upon and prepare a regular report to the fiduciary of the expenditures. This has worked exceptionally well for us on many cases. The key to success is clear, regular communications with the fiduciary about the expenditures *before* they are paid. After a short period, the fiduciary becomes comfortable with our decisions and we usually see them allow us to make the decisions for many of the ongoing services for the person, such as transportation, house maintenance, shopping, etc.

Case Study – We received a call all the way across the country from Maryland from a man named Sam regarding his brother, Don. Don was disabled and his health was deteriorating. Sam was the healthcare representative and power of attorney, but was unable to be with Don to coordinate care. Sam contacted an attorney who recommended he contact us for case management.

We worked with Sam for two years coordinating care and services to Don. We set up a trust account where Sam deposited $5,000 every other month for us to manage for Don. We coordinated doctor's visits, caregivers, transportation, and medicine management during the period.

Don had a commercial building and house that were in terrible condition. The commercial building had squatters that had to be removed. The place needed to be secured, cleaned up and sold. We coordinated all of the services and referred a realtor who sold the property in 60 days.

The house was worse. It was an expensive home in a great neighborhood in terrible shape. The house suffered from years of deferred maintenance and developed a serious and deadly mold condition. Personally, I believe Don's medical condition was partially a result of living in the mold infested house.

Sam knew the house needed repairs, but was not sure if the cost of the repairs would add enough value to the sale of the house to recoup the costs. We contacted several contractors and received bids for repairs. We had a realtor and appraiser provide reports of value before and after the anticipated repairs. They both said the repairs would raise the value of the home to recoup the costs, improve the salability of the house, and even provide additional profit.

We coordinated all of the repairs and the listing and sale of the house. Sam was elated. We made almost $50,000 more than he anticipated.

As Don's care continued to decline, we arranged facilities and moves to accommodate his care needs. When Don passed away, Sam was the personal representative responsible to settle the estate. We assisted with selling and distributing personal property as he directed. We arranged the burial needs and disposition of remains as he directed.

Sam recently contacted us two years after we closed the case with the following message: "I miss my Cornerstone friends."

As a case manager, the professional can do anything the fiduciary does with proper direction and delegation of authority or permission. Trust will soon develop between the professional and fiduciary. It is a win-win situation for everyone involved. Be sure to communicate well, be clear with direction, and ask questions if there is any doubt about any direction or action you are taking. Also, be sure to document, document, document all of your activity on the case.

Chapter 10
Ethics of a Professional Fiduciary

A fiduciary must be above reproach. The trust and integrity of the professional and layman fiduciary can be questioned at any time and must stand on its own merit. Not only can the ethics of any fiduciary be challenged, but civil liabilities exist with every case. That is why I included this chapter for your information.

I believe laymen fiduciaries should hold to the same ethical standards as professionals. I mean, the word 'fiduciary' means trust.

Without going into a deep debate, ethics is nothing more than determining right from wrong when making decisions related to services of a business or person. It is the guiding principle to every decision and action. Most decisions are easily determined between right and wrong. Ethics comes into play when a decision or action is questionable. Who really benefits? Is there an underlying motive for this action or decision? Whose interest is being met? Ethics is the measurement by which we insure every decision and action is for the benefit of the client, ward, or customer.

For example, if I hire a relative or friend to move a client, a question of ethics comes into play. Am I truly hiring the right person at the right price for the job so that the client benefits, or am I hiring someone I know for their benefit of getting paid? Ethics challenges us to review our decisions and actions for the benefit of the client.

Often, you, as a fiduciary, will be challenged with ethical questions or actions. It is your responsibility to make decisions and take actions that are not questioned. Err on the side of being ethical in all of your decisions.

One of the key elements of an ethical concern is a conflict of interest.

Conflicts of Interest

We explained earlier that a fiduciary is said to have a conflict of interest when the interest of the fiduciary conflicts with the interest of the principal, such that the decision making of the fiduciary is corrupted. A conflict of interest is a set of circumstances that creates a risk that professional judgement or actions regarding a primary interest will be unduly influenced by a secondary interest. Thus, the interests conflict with each other. The primary interest could be benefitting a relative by employing their services, as opposed to a secondary interest of obtaining the best service possible at the best rate for the protected person.

A conflict of interest exists if the circumstances are reasonably believed (on the basis of past experience and objective evidence) to create a risk that a decision _may_ be unduly influenced by other, secondary interests, and not on whether a particular individual is actually influenced by a secondary interest. It is the _perception_ of a conflict that matters; not the actual conflict or action of one.

Many states have written into their statutes and rules regarding fiduciaries and conflicts of interest. In Oregon, the rules and definitions are extensive.

Services - A fiduciary may employ a person in which the fiduciary has a pecuniary or financial interest _only_ after disclosing the nature of the interest to the court if the person is employed for the purpose of providing direct services to the protected person or for the purpose of providing services to the fiduciary that directly affect the protected person. Before the person is employed, the fiduciary must provide the court with the following:

(a) A full and accurate disclosure of the pecuniary or financial interest of the fiduciary in the person.

(b) A full and accurate disclosure of the services to be performed by the person.

(c) A full and accurate disclosure of the anticipated costs to the estate in using the person to provide the services.

In addition to the disclosures required, after making such inquiry as the court deems appropriate, the court may require additional disclosures for the purpose of assessing whether the pecuniary or financial interest of the fiduciary could compromise or otherwise affect decisions made by the fiduciary in carrying out the duties of the fiduciary.

The same requirements are mandated if the person to be employed does so through a business and not directly. The court requires all of the same disclosures and information *before the services can be performed or paid*. You can easily see that avoiding a conflict of interest while trying to get work done on a case can be challenging if the work is time sensitive, such as repairing a leaking roof.

This can also become problematic if the fiduciary uses their family members or friends to provide services to a protected person. My wife and I worked in the same company for almost twenty years, with both of us working on all of the cases. We made sure that all of our services were disclosed to the court through a standard disclosure before services were performed, and that detailed billings were submitted to the court requesting payment for our services. This is typical in a multi-fiduciary operation. It could be considered that we, as family members working together, would have a conflict of interest. If we take the definition at its core, we would never use anyone that we knew for any service to our protected persons, even if we knew they were less expensive, did better work, were trustworthy, and so on. We would only use people and contractors that we did not know, which is almost ludicrous.

Where it gets stickier is when we use a family member, like our children or other relative, to provide services to the protected person. Some of the services your child could possibly do are;

- Companion services – take the protected person shopping when no one else is available.
- Moving – sometimes a situation arises where the protected person needs to move right away. I might find myself asking my son to help me move them because no one else is available and we are under time constraints because of an event or emergency.
- Cleaning – Many times a place is in such terrible condition that we are unable to find someone to clean a property at a reasonable price.

- Simple maintenance, like cleaning gutters, mowing a lawn, repairing a small item around a house or apartment, hanging a television, and so on.
- Taking a client's car in for repairs.

And on and on and on.

You can see it is easy to ask a family member to do the task rather than try and track down a professional contractor or business person, but the court frowns greatly on this. We disclose to the court on every case that we use our son and friends to do work on many cases because he, or they, can do so at a lower rate, is more trustworthy, and has been fully vetted by us. Many of the courts have no problem with the disclosure or use of our family member or friend. Some courts do. The judge has the final say if we can use the person or not. In one county we don't even try and use him, even though by law we are allowed to do so with proper disclosure. You need to be wise with the battles you choose. The unfortunate result is that our client ends up paying more for a service than they need to. Check with your attorney on the best way to proceed regarding your situation.

Using a family member and paying more for their services than the market price is an obvious conflict of interest because your family member benefits at the expense of your client. This should _never_ be done.

Pecuniary Interest

A fiduciary has a pecuniary or financial interest in another person if the fiduciary, or any person related to, employed by or affiliated with the fiduciary has:

- Any direct or indirect ownership interest in the person;
- A business association with the person; or
- Any financial involvement with the person.

A fiduciary also has a pecuniary or financial interest in another person if the fiduciary, or any person related to, employed by or affiliated with the fiduciary, receives remuneration or any other financial benefit from the person, without regard to whether that remuneration or benefit is directly tied to the services provided to the fiduciary or protected person. This is a big statement. If you break it down, this means that the fiduciary has an interest if he or anyone he knows or is related to receive a financial benefit from anyone. That is pretty broad. If you take this at face value, I could not hire a contractor that I have used for ten years if he has done any free work for me or anyone I know. If he did anything at the office or home or on even on another case, like changing a fluorescent bulb, I could be perceived to have a conflict of interest if I used him on other cases. If you have benevolent friends or business associates, you could be at risk of being accused of having a conflict of interest. You can see how crazy this can get.

The key here is to disclose, disclose, disclose. Always be up front when you want to employ someone you are related to or know well. It makes sense to use someone you have worked with for many years because you know they will be on time, that they do good work, and that they will charge a reasonable rate. It is prudent to periodically compare their work and rates to another vendor to insure they are still competitive. Don't use just one vendor; mix it up a little.

If the court takes the position that the use of services of a particular person is a conflict, don't even try. Just find someone else and pay the higher price if you have to. Always check with your attorney.

Glossary

Affidavit - A written statement confirmed by oath or affirmation, for use as evidence in court.

ADL – Activities of Daily Living, such as bathing, eating, toileting, dressing, etc.

APS – Adult Protective Services – a government agency that investigates claims of abuse against vulnerable persons.

Advanced directives – A document that details a person's choices for end of life care and treatment.

Alzheimer's disease - Progressive mental deterioration that can occur in middle or old age, due to generalized degeneration of the brain. It is the most common cause of premature senility.

Attorney in fact – The person or party granted authority under a power of attorney.

Beneficiary - A person who derives advantage from something, especially a trust, will, or life insurance policy.

Best interest - The process of decision making by a surrogate decision maker regarding treatment for another person that most closely replicates what is the best decision for the person considering the facts.

Bond – Insurance for a specific purpose, such as mismanagement by a fiduciary resulting in a loss to the estate.

Capacity - The ability or power to do, experience, or understand something, such as the capacity to understand the implications of one's decisions.

Co-fiduciary – A fiduciary appointed along with one or more fiduciaries in the same capacity.

Competency - The mental ability of a person to understand the nature of their actions or a process.

Conflict of interest - A situation in which a person is in a position to derive personal benefit from actions or decisions made in their official capacity.

Conservatee – The person for whom a conservator is appointed over.

Conservator - A person who is legally responsible for managing the financial affairs of someone who is unable to manage their own affairs, especially an incompetent or disabled person.

Dementia - A chronic or persistent disorder of the mental processes caused by brain disease or injury and marked by memory disorders, personality changes, and impaired reasoning.

Devise - When an asset of an estate is specifically left, or given, to a person through a will or trust.

Donor - A person who donates or contributes, such as property to a trust.

Durable power of attorney – A power of attorney with broad powers that becomes effective when the principal becomes incapacitated.

Escheated – A process where a financial institution turns forgotten money or assets over to the state for holding and processing. If the asset is unclaimed after many years, the state takes possession of it. Each state has their own rules for escheating assets.

Executor - A person or institution appointed to carry out the terms of a will.

Fiduciary - [fi-**doo**-shee-er-ee] A person to whom property or power is entrusted for the benefit of another. One often in a position of authority who obligates himself or herself to act on behalf of another (as in managing money or property) and assumes a duty to act in good faith and with care, candor, and <u>loyalty</u> in fulfilling the obligation.

Financial power of attorney – A power of attorney regarding financial matters.

General power of attorney – A power of attorney with broad powers, including financial and healthcare, which terminates when the principal becomes incapacitated.

Grantor - A person who makes a grant or conveyance, such as property to a trust.

Guardian – A person who looks after and is legally responsible for someone who is unable to manage their own affairs, especially an incompetent or disabled person or a child whose parents have died.

Healthcare power of attorney – A power of attorney for healthcare.

Healthcare representative – A person granted authority under a healthcare power of attorney.

Incapable - Unable to behave rationally or manage one's affairs due to a medical condition or mental impairment; incompetent.

Income cap trust - A trust specifically designed for a person who receives monthly income above the Medicaid limit to receive property for their benefit without disqualifying them for Medicaid.

Informed consent –The process of gathering information buy a surrogate decision maker sufficient to make a decision regarding consent of treatment for another person.

Irrevocable trust – Inability to terminate or amend a trust document.

Intestate – The status of when a person dies and has no estate plan, thus the law must determine the distribution of the estate.

Letters of conservatorship – Documents issued by the court granting authority to a person or party to act as a conservator.

Letters of guardianship - Documents issued by the court granting authority to a person or party to act as a guardian.

Limited guardianship – A guardianship with limited authority or granted for a specific purpose.

Limited power of attorney –A power of attorney that is limited in scope and authority.

Medicaid – A state funded resource program that provides housing and medical care for persons with limited assets and income.

Mini mental test – A simple test of thirty questions that determines a person's cognitive abilities on a limited basis.

Pecuniary - Relating to or consisting of money.

Personal property – A person's property that is not real property, such as cars, furniture, collections, and clothes.

Personal representative - A person or institution appointed to carry out the terms of a will.

Petition - A formal written request appealing to authority with respect to a particular cause.

Pour over will – A will that 'pours over' or transfers assets that were left out of a trust, into a trust at the time of death of the beneficiary to be distributed and settled per the terms of the trust.

Power of attorney - The authority to act for another person in specified or all legal or financial matters; a legal document giving power of attorney to someone.

Prayer – The section of a motion or petition filed with the court asking what they want the court to do.

Principal – The person for whom another acts as an agent or representative.

Probate - The official proving and processing of a will.

Pro Bono – Working for free – no charge.

Protected person – A person for whom a guardian or conservator is appointed for.

Real property – Real estate, such as land and buildings.

Respondent – A person for whom a guardian or conservator has petitioned to be appointed for.

Revocable trust – Ability to terminate or amend a trust document.

Small estate – An estate small enough in the value of assets to not require a probate.

Special needs trust – A trust specifically designed for a disabled person to receive property for their benefit without disqualifying them for government benefits, such as Medicaid.

Springing power of attorney – A power of attorney that become effective upon an event.

Standing – A person who has a reason to be involved with a case before the court, such as a family member, close friend, involved professional, would be considered to have 'standing' before the court.

Substituted judgment – The process of decision making by a surrogate decision maker regarding treatment for another person that most closely replicates what the person would have wanted.

Supplemental needs trust - A trust specifically designed for a disabled person to receive property for their benefit without disqualifying them for government benefits, such as Medicaid.

Temporary guardianship – A guardianship appointed for a specific period of time.

Temporary power of attorney – A power of attorney that grants authority for a specific time period.

Trust - A legal document that places confidence in a party by making that party the nominal owner of property to be held or used for the benefit of one or more others.

Trustee - An individual person or party given control or powers of administration of property in trust with a legal obligation to administer it solely for the purposes specified.

Trustor – A person who creates a trust

Trust protector – A person or party who oversees the actions of a trustee in regards to managing a trust.

Vet – Vetting is the process of proving or researching something thoroughly.

Ward – A person under guardianship or conservatorship and oversight by the court.

Will - A legal document containing instructions as to what should be done with one's money and property after one's death.

Bibliography

http://www.dictionary.com/browse/fiduciary
https://www.merriam-webster.com/dictionary/fiduciary
http://penelope.uchicago.edu/Thayer/E/Roman/Texts/secondary/SMIGRA*/Fiducia.html
http://www.dictionary.com/browse/steward
Principal – one who appoints a fiduciary or has a fiduciary appointed on their behalf.
https://powerofattorney.com/oregon/general-power-attorney-oregon-form-adobe-pdf/
https://powerofattorney.com/wp-content/uploads/2013/07/oregon-medical-power-of-attorney-form.pdf
http://www.investopedia.com/terms/t/trust.asp
https://www.thelegacylawyers.com/faqs/what-are-the-parts-of-a-trust/
http://estate.findlaw.com/trusts/types-of-trusts.html
https://en.wikipedia.org/wiki/Uniform_Trust_Code
https://www.oregonlegislature.gov/bills_laws/ors/ors125.html
https://www.oregonlegislature.gov/bills_laws/ors/ors125.html
http://www.osbar.org/public/legalinfo/1117_probate.htm
https://www.google.com/search?-guardian
https://www.guardianship.org/wp-content/uploads/2017/07/NGA-Standards-with-Summit-Revisions-2017.pdf
https://en.wikipedia.org/wiki/Dementia
https://en.wikipedia.org/wiki/Dorothea_Puente